# ALLAN OCTAVIAN HUME, C.B

Owing to the antiquity and rarity of this book, certain pages are regrettably absent, and readability is compromised due to the blurring of the original text. If you possess any insights regarding the availability of these missing sections, kindly inform us. Your assistance is crucial in ensuring the completion of this significant work for the benefit of future generations.

# ALLAN OCTAVIAN HUME, C.B
## FATHER OF THE INDIAN NATIONAL CONGRESS,
## 1829 TO 1912

WILLIAM WEDDERBURN

GYAN

*Published by*

Gyan Publishing House
5, Ansari Road
Daryaganj, New Delhi-110002
Phone: 011-47034999, 9811692060
E-mail: books@gyanbooks.com

*Distribution Network*
gyanbooks.com
India, USA, Canada, UK, Australia



ISBN: 978-93-7133-009-1 (HB)
First Published, 1913

2nd Impression 2025

*Printed at:* Gyan Press, Delhi.



**ALLAN OCTAVIAN HUME, C.B**
Author William Wedderburn

# ALLAN OCTAVIAN HUME

# Allan Octavian Hume, C.B.

"Father of the Indian National Congress"

1829 TO 1912

BY

SIR WILLIAM WEDDERBURN, BART.

T. FISHER UNWIN
LONDON: ADELPHI TERRACE
LEIPSIC: INSELSTRASSE 20

# CONTENTS

# Contents

# ALLAN OCTAVIAN HUME

## (1829 TO 1912)

### INTRODUCTORY.

THE purpose of this brief memoir is to set forth the work and teaching of a man experienced in Indian affairs, who combined political insight with dauntless courage and untiring industry. The problem before him was, Can the continuance of British rule be made conformable to the best interests of the Indian people? And his answer was full of hope. Being firmly convinced that the interests of the Indian people and the British people were essentially the same, he believed that under a government in touch with popular feeling, the administration of India, within the British Empire, might be conducted with equal benefit to East and West, developing all that was best in the two great branches of the Aryan race.

But at the same time he realized with increasing anxiety, that the existing government, administered by foreign officials on autocratic lines, was dangerously out of touch with the people. He did not blame the men: the fault was in the system. There existed no recognized channel of communication between the rulers and the ruled; no constitutional means of keeping the official administrators informed regarding the condition, and feelings, and grievances of the people. There was therefore a great gulf fixed between the foreign bureaucracy, self-centred on the heights of Simla, and the millions painfully toiling in the plains below. And about the years 1878 and 1879, economic, in combination with political, troubles were actively at work throughout India ; the physical suffering of the many, acted on by the intellectual discontent of the few, was rapidly bringing popular unrest to the danger point. For the masses of the peasantry, scourged by poverty, famine, and pestilence, were beginning to give way to despair ; they could not make their voices heard, and they saw no hope of relief ; while, in the schools and colleges, the leaven of Western education was working among the intellectuals, teaching lessons of political history, and showing them how it was only through storm and stress that the British people had won for themselves the blessings of freedom. Hence the mind of the younger generation was stirred by vague dreams of revolutionary, and even violent, change. This critical condition of affairs was clearly understood by Mr. Hume. He had exceptional knowledge of what was going on below the surface ; and he knew that there was imminent risk of a popular outbreak, destructive of that peaceful progress upon which the welfare of India depends. The new wine was fermenting in the old bottles, and at any moment the bottles might burst and the wine be spilled. What was to be done ? Happily the solution of this fateful problem was ready to his hand. It was to be found in the simple formula of "Trust in the People." The Indian people, intelligent, law-abiding, the heirs of an ancient civilization, are worthy of the fullest trust ; and his urgent message to the British nation was this, that the path of safety lies in trusting them, and in associating them in the management of their own affairs.

# Allan Octavian Hume

The record of such a life must be of value to political thinkers among the British people, as teaching them how to fulfil a trust, such as never before has fallen to the lot of any nation. But specially it has seemed to me a duty to place before the youth of India the example of Mr. Hume's strenuous and unselfish life, and to bring into fresh remembrance the stirring words he uttered of encouragement and reproof, both alike prompted by his love of India, and his anxious care for her future. "Excelsior!" was his motto. His ideal was indeed a high one—the regeneration, spiritual, moral, social, and political, of the Indian people. But he taught that such a consummation could not be attained without the solid work-a-day qualities of courage, and industry, and self-denial.

## His Parentage and Early Years.

In order to realize the personality of Allan Hume, it is necessary to bear in mind his parentage, and his early surroundings. In the first place, he was the son of that sturdy and fearless Scottish patriot and reformer Joseph Hume, from whom it may be said that he inherited not only a political connection with India but also his love of science, and his uncompromising faith in democracy. The following character sketch is from the facile pen of the Rt. Hon. G. W. E. Russell: "Joseph Hume was born in 1777 and died in 1855. His father was a tradesman at Montrose: but the son preferred science to shopkeeping, and qualified as a surgeon. In 1796 he obtained an appointment in the service of the East India Company, and sailed for India. On the voyage the Purser fell sick; Hume took over his duties, and discharged them so well that the Company transferred him from marine to civil employment. He threw himself with ardour into the study of oriental languages, and acquired them so thoroughly that he was made an Interpreter, and in that capacity transacted a good deal of delicate and important business between the Company and the Native Powers. Those were the grand old days when Proconsuls became Nabobs, and the humblest officials in the service of the Company had frequent opportunities of indulging in the pastime of 'shaking the Pagoda Tree.' By 1808 Hume . . . had put by enough for his immediate object, which was to enter the House of Commons. . . . Willing the end, he willed the means, and, returning to England, he proceeded to buy one of the two seats which the Borough of Weymouth then possessed. The transaction was perfectly deliberate, straightforward and business - like. Hume drew his cheque, and the Free and Independent Electors of Weymouth undertook to return him for two parliaments. He was duly elected at a bye-election in January 1812, but a dissolution occurring in the following November, the vendors of the seat declined to fulfil their bargain, whereupon he brought an action for breach of contract, and recovered half his money. In 1818 he regained a seat in Parliament, this time for the Montrose Burghs, and he represented in turn Middlesex, Kilkenny, and again Montrose. He was a Radical of the deepest dye, and for thirty years was the recognized leader of the Radical group in Parliament. . . . It has always been the portion of Radicals to be dreaded and dispraised by the big-wigs of the Liberal party, and yet all the while to be tracing the path of advance along which, a few years later, the whole party advances to victory. This was as true of Joseph Hume as in later days of Bright and Cobden, of Mr. Chamberlain and Mr. Lloyd George. In 1834, amid universal derision, he attacked the Corn Laws, as producing artificial starvation, and declared for repeal. In 1835 he forced the attention of the House to the treasonable conspiracy which was masquerading under the name of Orangeism. He laboured for the extension of the suffrage, for the establishment of the ballot, and for the reform of ecclesiastical revenues. He moved for the abolition of sinecures and of flogging in the army. . . . But his special devotion was reserved for financial reform. It was at his suggestion that the word 'Retrenchment' was inserted between 'Peace' and 'Reform' in the official motto or war-cry of the Liberal party; and on all questions pertaining to finance, revenue, expenditure, and the like, he was the most pertinacious and unsparing of critics." But he did not forget India, while pursuing British reforms in every department; and on the second reading of Sir Charles Wood's Bill of 1853, to amend the Government of India, he spoke for several hours, championing the cause of the Indian people.

Sprung from such a stock, Allan Hume early displayed the characteristics of that hardy sea-faring race which peoples the north-east coast of Scotland.

As a lad his ambition was to enter the Royal Navy; and although he was destined for the Indian Civil Service, his father permitted him to "try the life"; and at the age of thirteen he joined the frigate *Vanguard* as junior midshipman, and served for a time, cruising in the Mediterranean. Later on, he was sent to the Training College at Haileybury, and on leaving, he took the opportunity to study medicine and surgery at University College Hospital, which was then adorned by the presence of the great surgeon Robert Liston. In 1849 he was duly posted to the Bengal Civil Service. Born in 1829, it is to be noted that his youth coincided with the years when, in all matters, social and political, the British nation was making a bound forward, under the impetus of the great Reform Movement of 1830, and when Bright and Cobden were triumphantly vindicating the right of the people to their daily bread.

## THE INDIAN CIVIL SERVICE.

We have now to follow him to India; and to record how he fared in the several stages of his official career. His period of service divides itself naturally into sections so diverse in their duties, that they may be treated almost as watertight compartments: (A) from 1849 to 1867, as a district officer; (B) from 1867 to 1870, as the head of a centralized department; (C) from 1870 to 1879, as a Secretary to the Government of India; and (D) June 1879, when he came into collision with the ruling authority, and practically ended his official career. In 1882 he resigned the service. Each of these sections carries a lesson of its own, for the personality of Mr. Hume acted as a touchstone, revealing the merits or demerits of each part of the administrative system: (A) as an executive officer, at the head of a great district in the North-West Provinces, he was a brilliant success. Both in peaceful times, and in the crisis of the Mutinies, his services at Etawah as an administrator deserved, and received, the cordial approval of the Government; and the official records show how, as regards (1) popular education, (2) police reform, (3) the liquor traffic, (4) the vernacular Press, (5) juvenile reformatories, and other domestic requirements, he laboured successfully as a pioneer of social progress. These years must have been among the happiest of his life; and the lasting results of his labours show how much may be accomplished for good by a district officer of the right sort, who understands the people, and is in full sympathy with them. It must however be noted that in those earlier years the serviceable activities of the district administration were not paralyzed, as they now are, by the iron grasp of the centralized departments. (B) As Commissioner of Customs he showed, notably in the matter of the great salt barrier, what useful work may be done by the head of a specialized department, which keeps to its own proper duties; and, as Director-General of Agriculture under Lord Mayo, he would have given fresh life to the distressed peasantry, had not sinister influences frustrated the scheme elaborated by that kindly Viceroy. (C) As Secretary to the Government of India, he had, for a while, his hand on the lever of the official mechanism. But (D), his career as a public servant was cut short, because he could not bend his principles to please the official faction at headquarters, known to the Indian public as the "Simla Clique." The sons of Zeruiah were too strong for him, and he was cast out from power. The great Indian bureaucracy is now about to give an account of its stewardship before a Royal Commission on the public service. In this national inquisition, the treatment accorded to Mr. Hume should be studied as an object lesson; and it will be for the official apologists to justify a system of administration which, in his case, forgot past services, disregarded proved competency, and penalized independence.

We may now proceed to note some of the leading matters illustrating the several sections of Mr. Hume's official life.

### (A) 1849 TO 1867, AS A DISTRICT OFFICER.

Mr. Hume's early official training is thus graphically described by the *Times of India*: "In those far-off days of the middle century the life and instruction of the young civilian differed in many respects from those of his successor to-day. He had less office work and less of European society; he was not so well equipped in theoretical knowledge, but he balanced the deficiency by a greater intimacy with the people he had to rule. Mr. Hume has himself described his early training. In the first month he had to take up the work of the Mohurrer or Clerk of the Police Station. Two or three months later he became Naib Darogha in another large thana, and then for a short period he had charge of a small thana as Thanadar. It was not until he had done all this that he was allowed to hear his first petty assault case. After the customary practical introduction into the routine of his varied duties, he became Assistant Magistrate and Collector, with special duties relating to dacoity investigations, and afterwards became Joint Magistrate and Deputy Collector at Etawah. This was the position he was holding when the Mutiny broke out." The method here described was a good healthy training for the young civilian, not at all calculated to produce a "sun-dried bureaucrat." Lord George Hamilton, when Secretary of State for India, complained that by the more modern system the district officials were deprived of the power of initiative, and taken out of touch with the people, being "so overburdened with correspondence, reports, and returns that they are really imprisoned in their offices for the greater part of the day." This result of over-centralization was not the system under which Mr. Hume was trained; he began at the foot of the official ladder, and worked his way up, learning by experience the duties of each of his subordinates, and in an open-air life, coming into direct contact with all classes of the people. Not that he was in any way deficient in "book learning," for it was partly to his superiority in the departmental examinations that he owed his rapid advancement to the position of responsibility which he occupied when the troubles began.

### *The Indian Mutiny.*

We now come to the sad and terrible events of the Mutiny of 1857; and I cannot do better than give *in extenso* the admirable summary of events at Etawah contributed to the journal *India* by his friend Colonel C. H. T. Marshall of the Indian Army, which shows how Mr. Hume, by the confidence he inspired among the people of his district, was able to save the lives of the European residents, to organize a force of faithful local levies, and finally to restore order, after defeating in a pitched battle a far superior force of disciplined mutineers, and capturing their six guns. The following is the account given by Colonel Marshall:—

"Allan Hume joined the Bengal Civil Service in 1849, towards the end of his twentieth year. Before he had been nine years in India, the great Mutiny of 1857 broke out, and he had many opportunities of showing his capabilities as a soldier as well as a civilian. He got rapid promotion; for though only twenty-six, he was officiating as Chief Civil Officer in charge of the Etawah District, in the North-West Provinces, with an area of 1693 square miles, a population of 722,000, and a revenue of £136,500. The headquarters were at the town of Etawah, which contained 34,000 inhabitants.

"When the fatal month of May 1857 opened, all was going smoothly—crime decreasing, revenue flowing in easily, the Great Canal spreading fertility through an ever-widening area, the railroad fast ripening. The community seemed happy and contented. The storm burst on the 10th, when the 3rd Cavalry mutinied at

Meerut, some two hundred and fifty miles to the north. Within two days the news reached Etawah and a small party of the mutineers appeared a day or so later. These were, after stout resistance, either captured or shot.

"What happened immediately after this is graphically told by Kaye in his work on the Sepoy Mutiny. He pays a fitting tribute to the subject of this article. He writes: 'The Magistrate and Collector was Mr. A. O. Hume, a son of the great English reformer, who had inherited the high public spirit and the resolute courage of his father.' He continues: 'On May 18th and 19th, another party of fugitives from the 3rd Cavalry appeared at Juswuntnuggur, ten miles from the town of Etawah. Being called upon to surrender by a patrol of police, they made a show of submission and then shot down their captors and took possession of a Hindu temple in a walled enclosure; there they prepared to defend themselves. When Hume heard of this he at once ordered his buggy, armed himself as best he could (with shot gun and revolver) and accompanied by his assistant, Mr. Daniell, started at 9 a.m. It was a blazing hot day and neither had broken his fast. On arriving, Hume invested the place with some irregular troopers and police. The difficulty was that the people were on the side of the mutineers. It was hopeless to assault, as they could obtain no support, on account of the great danger of storming. As the day passed, and the sun was setting, these two Englishmen, followed by only one policeman, made an effort to carry the place by themselves. The native was shot down and Daniell was shot through the face. Hume heroically got him away through the crowd to the carriage. They had killed one mutineer and mortally wounded another. The rebels escaped, during a storm, in the night.'

"Kaye adds: 'This was one of the first of those heroic

deeds of which I have before spoken . . . and bore noble witness to the courage and constancy of the national character. This English Magistrate and his assistant, in the face of an insurgent population, nobly strove to avenge themselves upon men who had a few days before murdered our own people.' They returned to Etawah, and 'for a while British authority as represented by Allan Hume was again in the ascendant.'

"The troops at Etawah still remained faithful; but not for long; for a few days later they also mutinied. They plundered the Treasury, burnt and looted the bungalows and released all the prisoners from the two jails. The ladies were got away safely to Agra Fort, escorted by loyal officials. The men remained at their posts trying to restore order. Mr. Hume began to raise local levies and hoped he might weather the storm, but all was in vain. News of disaster after disaster came in: the tide of the mutiny rose hourly, and by June 17 it was clear that the lives of none of the English there were safe, and that no good would result from their remaining at headquarters. They felt compelled to fall back upon Agra, and escaped during the night, reaching the Fort in safety.

"From the Agra Fort Hume kept in touch by correspondence (which was secretly conveyed) with the officials of his district, whom he knew to be still faithful. By proclamations and private letters he tried to let every one know the true state of things from the British point of view and to keep alive feelings of loyalty to the State.

"On July 5th a battle was fought at Agra. The rebel force consisted of two thousand of the best-drilled native soldiers with a troop of Bengal Horse Artillery. It was a sanguinary engagement in which many officers were killed. Hume was through it all serving with a battery. Colonel Patrick Bannerman, who, as a subaltern, was in the Fort with Hume (and is one of the few survivors), knew him well and admired his courage; he says he was one of the pluckiest men he had ever met. He was out in the open with the guns for several nights, until he was laid low by cholera and had to be sent back invalided to the Fort.

"As soon as he was fit for work he was most anxious to return to Etawah, but was not allowed to do so until December 30th, when he started, with Mr. G. B. Maconochie, his assistant, escorted by fifty of the 2nd Punjab Infantry, under Lieutenant Sheriff. He managed to re-occupy the town of Etawah on January 6th. Once there he lost no time in raising local levies. By the end of the month he had drilled 200 infantry and 150 cavalry; he also had five guns and fifty gunners. Later his force was strengthened by a detachment of Alexander's Horse.

"The position in Etawah was, however, very critical. They were twice threatened by a strong body of mutineers. On February 7, 1858, an action was fought at Anuntram, twenty-one miles from Etawah, in which Hume greatly distinguished himself. The rebels, some twelve or thirteen hundred in number, with one gun, were very strongly posted in a large grove of mango-trees with a six-foot wall all round and a small ditch in front and a village on their left. The attacking force were sixty troopers of Irregular Horse, under Captain Alexander, some three hundred matchlock men, and eighty Sowars of the Local Horse, with Mr. Hume and Mr. Maconochie. They had also one 3-pounder brass gun. It will be sufficient for the purpose of this article to record the following extracts from official reports.

"From Captain Alexander to Brigadier Seaton: 'Mr. Hume, having with some difficulty collected about two or three hundred matchlock men out of the 700, advanced most gallantly with them towards the entrenchment; the fire of the enemy had been directed towards my troop, but seeing the advance of our matchlock men, turned it towards them; our gun then opened, advancing nearer each discharge. About the fifth discharge our gun was close up to the wall, and a rush being made, headed in the most gallant manner by Mr. Hume, the enemy began to retreat. A copy of Mr. Hume's report to Government is enclosed . . . and shows the active and gallant part taken by that officer and his matchlock men.'

"The Commander-in-Chief, in reporting to the Governor-General (Lord Canning), requests that he may 'bring to the special notice of his Lordship the extremely gallant conduct of Mr. Hume and Captain Alexander.'

"The Governor-General's reply is, that he 'has great satisfaction in publishing for general information the subjoined reports of an action fought with the rebels at Anuntram on the 7th instant by Alexander's Horse and a body of Zemindaree troops led by Mr. A. O. Hume, Magistrate of Etawah, the whole under the command of Captain Alexander. The Governor-General entirely concurs with his Excellency the Commander-in-Chief in considering this affair to reflect the highest credit on Captain Alexander and Mr. Hume, as well as Mr. Maconochie, who, with conspicuous bravery and cool determination, led their men against the very superior number of the rebels and obtained a signal victory over them.'

"The result of this action was that 131 of the rebels were killed, their gun, ammunition, baggage, ponies, and arms were captured. Hume, in his own report, says: 'The pursuit over, we returned with the captured gun to

Etawah, having accomplished the whole affair, including the fifty miles' ride, in twelve hours.'

"During the following six months Hume was constantly at work in the field against the rebels escaping from Oudh. One or two extracts may here be given from his final report when the pacification of the District had been accomplished :—

"'On April 21 we made a most successful cavalry attack on a party of Roop Singh's at Ajeetmul, and though the enemy were in great force all round, drove them with the loss of seven men helterskelter into the ravines. The audacity of this attack, for the time, completely frightened the rebels. Next day, by a very pretty combined movement from two directions, we surprised the enemy, cut up fifteen, took prisoner and hung three. . . . Mr. C. Doyle was shot through the right shoulder.'

"In the May following there came a series of desperate operations on the banks of the Jumna against Feroze Shah, of the Delhi royal family. 'Of this,' wrote Hume, 'it is sufficient here to say that in an open boat in the middle of May (with a force of 410 horse and foot, and two 3-pounders) we in seven days collected and raised (often under the enemy's fire) 36 boats, and after many skirmishes and a pitched battle (in which we defeated a far superior force of the mutineers, taking the whole of their six guns, all their baggage, and killing eighty-one regular sepoys), safely conveyed them 63 miles down the river, past hostile villages and forts.'

"By the end of the year the District of Etawah was once more at peace; and in closing the notes on this important stage of Hume's career, no better summary of the work he did can be given than by quoting some of his remarks at the end of his report :—

"'No District in the North-West Provinces has, I believe, been more completely restored to order. None in which so few severe punishments have been inflicted. Mercy and forbearance have, I think I may justly say, characterized my administration. . . . We had before us then a great and glorious problem to solve, viz., how to restore peace and order and the Authority of Government with the least possible amount of human suffering.'

"There can be no doubt that his statesmanlike tact, his brilliant courage and tenacity of purpose made it easier for him than it would have been for many others to restore confidence among the people and evolve peace and order out of chaos.

"He did not receive his reward until 1860, when he was created a Companion of the Bath. Little enough reward was it for his great services. But those days were different from the present day, when honours and decorations are thrown broadcast among the deserving and the undeserving alike."

Let us now proceed to review some of his most notable work for the peace and progress of his district.

### (1) *Popular Education.*

In a detailed report dated 21st January 1857, Mr. Hume describes, as follows, the circumstances under which he initiated his system of free schools in Etawah: "In February last I received semi-official permission to attempt the establishment of Elementary Free Schools, to be supported by a voluntary cess, contributed by the landed proprietors. After no little opposition had been overcome by patient argument and perseverance, a large majority of the Zemindars of Pergunnah Etawah consented to the levy of the cess; and they having formally declared the same at a great public meeting held for the purpose, and paid up the first instalment of their subscription, 32 schools were opened on the 1st of April, in the more important villages of the Pergunnah." These proceedings were approved by the Lieutenant-Governor, by the Government of India, and subsequently by the Court of Directors. Encouraged by this auspicious beginning, this system (known as the "Hulqabundee" system) was gradually extended to the whole of the District, and by the 1st of January 1857, 181 schools had been established, with 5186 scholars (including 2 girls) on the lists. As regards school buildings, the beginning was made in a humble but effective way: "Only three buildings and these 'cutcha' ones have yet been erected for the schools. At present these are chiefly located in some commodious apartment of the Zemindar (if he is popular) or in some till-lately ruined house, repaired after a fashion by the villagers. Nevertheless cleanliness is enjoined, and attained; and every school has been furnished with thick carpetings, sufficient to accommodate the teacher and all his pupils." It was hoped that later on neat and permanent buildings for the larger schools would be erected from surplus school funds, but in the meantime no financial alarms were allowed to impede the opening of a school where accommodation could be found sufficient to meet the modest requirements of village life. For the 181 schools teachers were found (8 on Rs. 6 per mensem, 39 on Rs. 5, and 134 on Rs. 4), many of them "for the pay they receive very able men"; and detailed rules were printed in Hindee and Oordoo, prescribing the course of study, the duties of teachers, and the arrangements to secure a strict and consistent supervision. But early in this movement, a want was felt for some institution which should serve as a stepping stone for the scholars from the elementary schools to the Agra College; and accordingly on the 1st of August 1856 Mr. Hume opened at Etawah a Central English and vernacular school, as the germ of such an institution. Here too he met with opposition; but this was overcome, and by the 1st of January 1857 there were 104 students in attendance. One step more remained—the foundation of scholarships in connection with the Central School, for the maintenance of a few of the best of these students, during the completion of their education in the Agra College. One such scholarship he recommended to the Government in memory of his lamented friend and coadjutor Koour Ajeet Sing; another he proposed to found himself; and he hoped that some of the local gentlemen might in this matter be induced to follow his example.

Upon this happy development of peace and progress the Mutiny of May 1857 fell like a thunderbolt. Yet, after two years, when order had been re-established, Mr. Hume was able to report, on the 25th of January 1859, that his system of education was again in active life: "This system even the past revolution failed to obliterate; some of the schools remained open from first to last, and now though it is but a few months since we finally regained possession of the whole district, the schools are once more numbered by hundreds, the scholars by thousands." Unfortunately, following the Mutiny, official opinion appears to have suffered a reaction on the question of popular education, and he expressed his concern that many "entirely disapprove of any efforts to cultivate the native mind; many condemn, as unconditionally, a merely secular education." In this report, therefore, of January 1859 he vindicated the policy of enlightenment, declaring that "assert its supremacy as it may at the bayonet's point, a free and civilized government must look for its stability and permanence to the enlightenment of the people, and their moral and intellectual capacity to appreciate its blessings." The reactionary spirit showed itself shortly afterwards in a

Government Circular of 28th January 1859, in which objection was taken to the employment of native agency for the promotion of education, and the Collector was warned not to attempt to persuade the people to send their children to the schools or to contribute to the maintenance. Against these orders Mr. Hume, in a letter of 30th March 1859, respectfully, but earnestly protested, pointing out that the Court of Directors had directed officers "to aid with all the influence of their high position the extension of education." He further explains, in considerable detail, why he believes that it is through the influence of their own leaders that the people can best be convinced of the benefits of education; and he concludes on a personal note of deep pathos: "I cannot," he says, "but found hopes of indulgence on the intense interest that I feel in the subject, and the ceaseless attention that I have paid it. For years past it has been *the* dream of my leisure moments, *the* object of my hopes, and although I have *achieved* little as yet, I cannot as I watch the feeble beginnings avoid recalling an alpine scene of happy memories, when I saw the first drops of a joyous stream trickling through the huge avalanche that had so long embayed it, and feeling confidence from that augury that day by day and month by month that tiny rill gathering strength and size will work out its resistless way, and at last dissipating the whole chilling mass of ignorance, the accumulations of ages, pass on unobstructed to fertilize and enrich an empire. History, alas! presents us with too many examples of the long obstructed stream hurling aside at last roughly its opposing barriers and sweeping onwards an ungovernable flood heaping up desolation where it should have scattered flowers. Let it be ours to smooth and not impede its path, ours not by cold explanations of policy but by enlisting the sympathies and affections of the people in the cause, to watch and direct its progress and turn it, under God's blessing, to good, and good alone." The documents at my disposal do not state what, at the time, was the effect of this passionate appeal. But the whole episode, showing how gallantly, under the most difficult circumstances, the battle was fought more than half a century ago, should hearten those who have now taken it in hand to emancipate their poorer brethren from the bonds of ignorance, by making elementary education not only free but compulsory.

### (2) *Police Reform.*

In 1860 Government issued orders to reorganize the police in accordance with the recommendations of the Police Commission, and Police Superintendents were appointed for each District, to act under the orders of an Inspector-General of Police. By the 1st of January 1861 the Etawah police were reorganized by Mr. Hume, as directed. But, having duly carried out the orders of Government, he felt it his duty (see his despatch of March 1861) to report his belief that the new system was "defective in principle," "impracticable in its chief provision," and, with few exceptions, "a change for the worse." Briefly stated, his objections were, that the system failed to secure the severance of police and judicial functions; that it created a divided responsibility between the Police Superintendent and the District Magistrate; and that the Police Superintendents, on whom practically devolved the work of criminal investigations, were destitute both of local experience and of local influence. His remedy was that the Chief Civil Officer of the District (the "Collector") should represent the Executive Government in all departments, including the police; but that neither he nor his subordinates should exercise any magisterial powers whatever. The police duties should, he considered, be performed by the several grades of the Collector's subordinates, men well in touch with the population, and possessing influence as representing the supreme authority in all departments; while the Collector, as head of the District police, should be responsible, through the Inspector-General, to the Government for the repression of crime and the general peace of his District. The ordinary magisterial work of the District would be entrusted to Honorary Magistrates and Subordinate Judges of the various grades, working under a Stipendiary Magistrate, from whom an appeal would lie to the Sessions Judge. This scheme provided for the complete separation of police and judicial functions which still remains a pressing need at the present day; and it must also strongly commend itself to those who hold that the Collector should be the responsible embodiment of the "Sirkar," in all branches of the administration within his own district, and lament the present destruction of his authority by the encroachments of the centralized departments.

### (3) "*Abkaree*"—*The* "*Wages of Sin.*"

Similarly, as regards the Liquor Traffic, he reported, 14th September 1860, that the orders of the Government had been carried out, producing an increase of receipts, Rs. 1858 in excess of the previous year, and Rs. 5251 in excess of the average collections of the past ten years; but at the same time he did not hesitate to express, in the strongest terms, his abhorrence of such a source of revenue: "Financially speaking," he wrote, "bearing in mind the almost unexampled distress in the face of which this settlement was concluded, it may be regarded as eminently successful. To me however the constant growth of the Abkaree revenue is a source of great regret. Year after year, but alas in vain, I protest against the present iniquitous system which first produced and now supports a large class whose sole interest it is to seduce their fellows into drunkenness and its necessary concomitants, debauchery and crime. Unfortunately these tempters are too successful, and year by year the number of drunkards and the demand for drugs and spirituous liquors increases. Those only who like myself take great pains to ascertain what goes on amongst the native community, really have any conception of the frightful extent to which drunkenness has increased during the last twenty years. Moreover, while we debauch our subjects we do not even pecuniarily derive any profit from their ruin. Of this revenue, the wages of sin, it may in the words of the old adage be truly said that illgotten wealth never thrives, and for every rupee additional that the Abkaree yields, two at least are lost to the public by crime, and spent by the Government in suppressing it. I fear that it is useless saying more now on this subject—for five years I have yearly but without avail protested against the present system, and though I at this moment see no hopes of reform, I have no doubt whatsoever that if I be spared a few years longer I shall live to see effaced in a more Christian-like system one of the greatest existing blots on our government of India. I trust that this letter may be submitted in full to the Board." Sad to say, after half-a-century this "greatest existing blot" still remains uneffaced.

### (4) "*The People's Friend.*"

Mr. Hume, looking forward to coming years, had a special care for the young, both for the docile and the wayward. Each year the schools were turning out boys and youths, able to read, and with their intelligenee awakened, but the only books in their own language were scarce and dear, and for the most part neither instructive nor edifying. He therefore, in co-operation with his friend Koour Lutchman Sing, determined to supply this want; and towards the end of 1859 they started *The People's Friend*, a vernacular paper, carefully conducted, and published at so cheap a rate as to be accessible to the poorest of the village youths. It was intended originally for Etawah alone, but its fame went abroad, and it circulated throughout the North-West Provinces, and even penetrated to Gwalior and Bhurtpore. Not being an official publication it did not come under the suspicion of partiality, and rendered valuable service in explaining the policy of the Government, and in counteracting influences prejudicial to good feeling. The Government of the North-West Provinces subscribed for six hundred copies, and *The People's Friend* came under the favourable notice of the Viceroy, at whose suggestion copies of the paper were forwarded, with translations, to the Secretary of State, for submission to Queen Victoria. It was felt that Her Gracious Majesty would be interested in seeing this early specimen of Indian journalism, and in realizing the gratitude and affection inspired by her personality among the humblest and most distant of her subjects.

### (5) *Juvenile Reformatories.*

And the bad boys had to be remembered as well as the good boys. It appears that the Etawah District was periodically invaded by bands of professional young thieves, coming from certain outside tracts. They were dealt with by the police, brought before the magistrates, and were punished by flogging and imprisonment. They thus became thoroughly hardened, and eventually ripened into dacoits and receivers of stolen property. Evidently there was need for special treatment of this class; and as early as 1863 Mr. Hume pressed for the establishment of a Juvenile Reformatory, where these boys would be separated from adult criminals, and given a chance of amendment by discipline, by instruction, and by training in useful industries. At first the Supreme Government did not favour the proposal for reformatories, and preferred that separate accommodation should be provided in the central jails for juvenile criminals. But in 1867 Mr. Hume returned to the charge, and being supported by the Lieutenant-Governor of the North-West Provinces, he submitted (2nd September 1867) a detailed scheme for a Juvenile Reformatory on a desirable site close to Etawah. He was fortunate in having the sympathy of Dr. Clark the Inspector-General of Prisons, and of Dr. Sherlock the Superintendent of the Jail, a very valuable coadjutor, who volunteered to take charge of the Reformatory in addition to his other duties. The system proposed was that known as the Irish system; the building was to be circular and radiating; and as the scheme was experimental, he proposed that a beginning should be made with one "sector," equal to one-fourth of the circular building. This could be ready by the 1st of January 1868 for the reception of one hundred boys, the expense for building this portion being Rs. 11,000, and the cost of maintenance Rs. 464 per mensem. The idea was that the Divisions of Agra and Allahabad would produce yearly about one hundred boy convicts, and that in each of the three following years another sector should be built to receive them. As the term of retention would usually be four years, it was calculated that by the 1st of January 1871 the first sector would be vacated, and ready to receive the boy criminals belonging to that year. When completed the cost of the whole building would be Rs. 35,000, and maintenance Rs. 1250 per mensem. This scheme was cordially approved by the Government of the North-West Provinces, and forwarded for sanction to the Government of India.

There are other valuable reports on special subjects. For example, there is a long letter on cotton cultivation and supply, dated 24th July 1860, in reply to questions from Mr. Haywood, Secretary to the Cotton Supply Association of Manchester. This letter cannot be condensed or summarized, but it is so full of interesting facts; it is so perfect a model of what such a report should be; and the subject is so important at the present day, that it is reproduced *in extenso*, Appendix I. Again, there is a treatise, dated 1865, covering twenty closely printed pages, on "Canal irrigation in its relation to the Permanent Settlement"; but the subject is very technical, and the examples of his administrative work already given must suffice, as showing the wide scope of his activities, and the infinite patience with which his facts were collected and recorded. It is pleasant to find that his District management again and again received commendation from the higher authorities. As regards the police administration the Lieutenant-Governor congratulated him on "the extinction of the crime of affray in the once turbulent District of Etawah. It is also satisfactory to find that owing to that officer's influence and exertions, the crime of female Infanticide, once so prevalent, is now of rare occurrence in the District, and that no less than 173 outlaws have been apprehended during the year"; and the Government, in its Order of 13th November 1860, recorded as follows its appreciation of his work and character: "To much administrative ability, and great powers of sustained exertion, he adds a cordial interest in the prosperity of his District, and the welfare of its people, and sacrifices all personal considerations to the conscientious discharge of his duty." Again, in Government Resolution of 8th March 1861 it was recorded that "The Lieutenant-Governor has derived much satisfaction from his visit to the District of Etawah, and desires to place on record his acknowledgment of the ability, energy, and judgment with which its administration is conducted by Mr. Hume."

## (B) 1867 TO 1870. COMMISSIONER OF CUSTOMS.

With so distinguished a record as a District Administrator, it is not surprising that Mr. Hume was selected to be the head of one of the great centralized departments; and in July 1867 he was appointed Commissioner of Customs for the North-West Provinces. In this capacity his principal achievement was the gradual abolition of the vast Customs barrier, 2500 miles long, which had hitherto been kept up to protect the Government salt monopoly by excluding the cheap salt produced in the Rajputana States. This grotesque fortification, guarded along its whole length like the Great Wall of China, extended west to east across the continent of India, from Attock on the Upper Indus to near Cuttack on the Bay of Bengal. It was the source of wasteful expense, corruption, and great inconvenience to the public; and the proposal for its abolition was of long standing, having received the approval of successive Governors-General; but action had been always postponed because of the difficulties connected with the negotiation of a series of treaties with numerous Native

States. These treaties were successfully negotiated by Mr. Hume; and the Secretary of State cordially recognized the value of his services, writing as follows to the Viceroy (Despatch No. 3 of 6th February 1879): "I entirely concur in the high appreciation of Mr. Hume's long and valuable services expressed by your Excellency's Government; for to him, as you observe, is due the initiation, prosecution, and completion of that policy which has led to the agreements entered into with the several States concerned." In a letter from Mr. Hume to the Press some interesting particulars are given as to the merits of the award, under which the Sambhur Lake and other sources of salt supply were transferred from the Rajputana States to the British Government. On the one hand it had been contended that the amount awarded as compensation was mean and insufficient; on the other hand he had been severely taken to task for his supposed reckless liberality. As regards the allegation of insufficiency, Mr. Hume points out that the two States chiefly concerned were Jeypore and Jodhpore, and under the award Jeypore received double the amount realized in previous years, while Jodhpore received three lakhs more than it ever did before. On the other hand, as regards the claims of the Government, Mr. Hume's award was accepted and confirmed by Lord Mayo and Sir John Strachey, the Minister of Finance; and if the liberality to the Rajput States seemed at the time excessive, it was justified by the ultimate results; for by the employment of scientific methods, the Government became a gainer financially from the transaction; while the public was much benefited: where 1½ millions of maunds were before produced, 5 millions were now brought into the market, so that for Rs. 3 annas 2 per maund a better article was procurable than that for which Rs. 6 and 7 was previously paid.

## *An Agricultural Department.*

But while thus engaged in large transactions for the benefit of the public revenue, his anxious thought continued always to be for the welfare of the peasant cultivators; and fortunately his views met with the fullest sympathy from Lord Mayo, who became Governor-General in 1869. Lord Mayo was himself a practical agriculturist; he had indeed farmed for a livelihood, and made a living out of it: "Many a day," he used to say, "have I stood the livelong day in the market selling my beasts." Hitherto the attention of the Government had been chiefly directed to collecting the revenue, and little had been done to develop agricultural resources; more energy had been applied to shearing the sheep than to feeding him. Lord Mayo, as an expert, understood the fatal consequences of such a policy; and in consultation with Mr. Hume, proposed to provide a remedy, by organizing the agricultural department on a business footing as a genuine Bureau of Agriculture, and placing it under a competent Director-General, with a free hand to work out the salvation of rural India.

In a pamphlet entitled "Agricultural Reform in India," published in 1879, Mr. Hume gives particulars of this scheme, which proposed to make the Director-General of Agriculture a whole-time officer, supreme in his own department, and only nominally attached for official purposes to the Secretariat: "The Director-General was to have immediately under him a small staff of experts, and was to keep up only just such an office as was absolutely unavoidable. There was to be as little writing and as much actual work as possible. Directors of Agriculture were to be appointed in each Province, also to be aided by experts. They were to work partly through the direct agency of farms and agricultural schools, and partly through the revenue officials of all grades down to the village accountants." It was an open secret that Lord Mayo regarded Mr. Hume as an ideal Director-General of Agriculture; and no one can read this pamphlet without seeing how intimately he had studied the peasant cultivators, on whose behalf he was striving—their merits and their shortcomings, their difficulties, and the remedies to be applied. The tradition and experience of three thousand years have given them minute knowledge with regard to their own ancestral holdings; and he points out that they know to a day when it is best to sow each staple and each variety of each staple; they accurately distinguish every variety of soil, and the varying properties and capacities of each; they fully realize the value of manures; they know the advantages of deep ploughing, and thoroughly pulverizing the soil; but they also realize where, with a scanty supply of manure, it would be folly to break the shallow-lying pan: "As for weeds, their wheat-fields would, in this respect, shame ninety-nine hundredths of those in Europe." "So far therefore as what may be called non-scientific agriculture is concerned, there is little to teach them. . . . On the other hand, we must not overrate their knowledge; it is wholly empirical, and is in many parts of the country, if not everywhere, greatly limited in its application by tradition and superstition. . . . So, then, it is not only external disadvantages against which the Indian cultivator has to contend, it is not only that his knowledge is still in the primary experience stage, but that even this knowledge is often rendered of no avail by the traditions of an immemorial religion of agriculture." In the Appendix to his Pamphlet are given a number of quaint couplets, current in Upper India, which record the traditional prognostications with regard to each of the "Nakhats," or subdivisions of the Zodiac. The twelve Nakhats which fill the critical period between the 23rd of May and the 4th of November, are the most important for the cultivator, and indicate good or evil influence with regard to sowings, harvestings, and the seasonableness of the rainfall. The obstacles to progress caused by superstition and the belief in omens and divinations will, it is hoped, give way before rural education, especially if it is free and compulsory. But the troubles of the cultivator arising from more material causes, form the main difficulty in the case: his want of capital for irrigation and manure, his bondage to the moneylender, the grievous mortality among the plough-cattle. As regards this last point, Mr. Hume feelingly describes the tragedy of these faithful and beautiful friends of man: "Over a great portion of the Empire, the mass of the cattle are starved for six weeks every year. The hot winds roar, every green thing has disappeared, no hot weather forage is grown, the last year's fodder has generally been consumed in keeping the well-bullocks on their legs during the irrigation of the spring crops, and all the husbandman can do is just to keep his poor brutes alive on the chopped leaves of the few trees and shrubs he has access to, the roots of grass and herbs that he digs out of the edges of fields, and the like. In good years he just succeeds; in bad years the weakly ones die of starvation. But then come the rains. Within the week, as though by magic, the burning sands are carpeted with rank luscious herbage, the cattle *will* eat and overeat, and *millions* die of one form or other of cattle disease, springing out of this starvation, followed by sudden repletion with rank, juicy, immature herbage." Mr. Hume estimated the average annual loss of cattle in India by preventible cattle disease at fully ten million beasts, roughly valued at £7,500,000. "And be it noted that it is not only the supply of manure that this fearful mortality amongst the cattle, and their resulting paucity, so greatly restricts; it is the little hoarded capital of the peasant, the very mainspring of agriculture in India, that is thus flung away." Village plantations for fodder, the establishment of Veterinary Colleges, the spread of useful information among the people, and other well considered measures, organized by a competent Agricultural Department; these were the practical remedies advocated by Mr. Hume: "The Indian climates, varying as these do, appear to be specially favourable to cattle. Every one who has kept cattle here knows that if moderately fed, and given plenty of work, and kept away from contagion, they never seem to be sick or sorry, but work on, hardy and healthy, from youth to extreme old age. They are very prolific too. If our poor beasts had only reasonably fair play, the whole Empire would swarm with cattle, and cattle able to work the heaviest ploughs, and, in soils and situations where this was necessary or desirable, to plough as deep as you like."

He held the Civil Courts in the rural districts directly responsible for the bondage of the cultivators to the moneylender; and he recommended that rural debt cases should be disposed of summarily, and finally, on the spot by selected Indians of known probity and intelligence, who should be "sent as judges from village to village, to settle up, with the aid of the village elders, every case of debt of the kind referred to, in which any one of its inhabitants was concerned." The expected result is thus graphically described: "These judges would be fettered by no codes and no forms of procedure, and they would hear both parties' stories *coram populo*, on the village platform of the debtor's own village. It is needless to tell any one who knows the country that while, when you get him into court, no witness seems to be *able* to tell the truth, on his own village platform, surrounded by his neighbours, no villager in personal questions like these seems able to tell an untruth. Everybody knows everybody else's affairs; let the speaker deviate perceptibly from the *facts*, and immediately out go tongues all round, and jeers and cries of 'Wah,' 'Wah,' remind him that he is *not* in court, and that that kind of thing will not go down at home." In 1879 a detailed scheme on these lines was formulated for the benefit of the distressed Deccan ryot, but it was disallowed by the Bombay Government.

These brief extracts show how fully he was in sympathy with the ryot, and how peculiarly his past experience had qualified him to direct the work of agricultural reform. But in addition to this, he possessed scientific qualifications: he was well versed in practical European agriculture; he was conversant with the more modern German and English writings on agriculture, both theory and practice; and he had, for his own information and amusement, farmed in an experimental way throughout his many years of service in India as a District Officer. Moreover, at this time he was residing with Lord Mayo, and had discussed repeatedly with him all the details of his scheme. Add to this Mr. Hume's boundless energy and enthusiasm, and we can see what a hopeful prospect would have been opened out for the relief of the peasantry, and the development of the State's interest in the land, had he been placed at the head of a genuine Agricultural Bureau.

Unhappily, Lord Mayo was not able to carry out his scheme. Adverse influences, too powerful to resist, arose both at Simla and at the India Office in London. To meet financial objections, Lord Mayo modified his scheme, to its serious detriment. Yet even this modified scheme "was met with perhaps the most strenuous opposition any long-considered project of a Viceroy, himself a practical expert in the particular subject, ever encountered, and when at the last the Department was created, it had lost every one of the essential characters on which its possible success as a Bureau of Agriculture was absolutely dependent." This sinister and unreasoning obstruction reminds one of the bitter complaint of Sir Louis Mallet, when Permanent Under Secretary at the India Office in 1875. In a minute, printed in the report of the Famine Commission of 1880, he wrote: "I am compelled to say that, since I have been connected with the India Office, I have found just as strong a repugnance to the adoption of any adequate measures for the collection of a comprehensive and well-digested set of facts, as to the recognition of general principles"; and he instanced "the vehement opposition of some members of Council" to his advocacy of Dr. Forbes Watson's proposals for an industrial survey in India. The treatment accorded to Lord Mayo calls to mind how similar obscurantist counsels prevailed in 1884, when the scheme for Agricultural Banks, recommended unanimously by Lord Ripon's Government, and approved by public opinion in India and in England, was stabbed to death in the dark when it entered the portals of the India Office.

### (C) 1870 TO 1879, AS SECRETARY TO THE GOVERNMENT OF INDIA.

As Lord Mayo was unable to carry out his scheme for a real working Agricultural Bureau, he had to content himself with making agriculture one of the subjects included in a miscellaneous department of the Secretariat, entitled the Department of Revenue, Agriculture, and Commerce. In July 1871 he appointed Mr. Hume as Secretary in this Department, on account of his special knowledge of agriculture, transferring him from the Home Department, where he had been acting as Secretary for a year. At the same time he changed the designation of the Department, putting Agriculture before Revenue; but to this the Secretary of State took exception, and in his Despatch of 3rd August 1871, directed that in the title of the Department "Revenue," as the subject of paramount importance, should come first. At the same time he laid down the rule that "the officer appointed to the post of Secretary in this Department, should always be chosen on account of his knowledge of the subjects connected with revenue, rather than from any knowledge which he may possess of agricultural or commercial matters." Agriculture had therefore to take a back seat; and upon this conclusion Mr. Hume remarks, "It will be seen, therefore, that as constituted, this Department never was, and never was intended by the Home Government to be, a Department of Agriculture. Lord Mayo hoped to convert it into this, but with his death India lost the warmest, most competent, and at the same time, most influential advocate for agricultural reform. No change, such as he contemplated, has ever been made in the constitution of the Department, and succeeding administrations have only made the official bonds more rigid, and converted its chief more and more thoroughly into a mere desk-tied secretary." It was reserved for a later generation to realize that improved agriculture is the backbone of Indian finance.

Though deeply disappointed by the frustration of Lord Mayo's scheme, Mr. Hume did not on that account relax his efforts. He was a workman of the sort that, if refused the tools of his choice, will make the best of the tools he can get; and accordingly he admitted that, "Although circumstances had deprived Lord Mayo's new department of all claim to be considered an Agricultural Bureau, its formation marked an era in the history of the country, and served a most useful purpose. In it were gathered up into one homogeneous whole numberless branches of the administration, all more or less potential factors in the material progress of the Empire." Manfully therefore did he strive, during the years he remained a Secretary, to put fresh life into the operations of the various branches of the administration which came under his control. Besides matters directly pertaining to Agriculture and Horticulture, he had to deal with Forestry, including the conservation of existing forests, the "reboisment" of denuded tracts, and the supply of timber and firewood to the public; Surveys, with explorations for minerals; Fisheries, including the publication of Dr. Day's scientific manual of Indian fishes; Emigration and Migration; Meteorological observations, museums, and exhibitions of art and industry; merchant shipping, harbours, lighthouses, and pilotage; Inland Customs, including salt; and Sea Customs, including the tariff of import and export duties. But among these multitudinous and distracting claims on his attention, Mr. Hume's thoughts were always primarily for the humble ryot, and his need for water supply, manure, developed products, improved implements; and Note B of his Pamphlet on Agricultural Reform furnishes a record of carefully collected facts, with special information and advice, supplied in handy form to the rural population.

## (D) 1879 TO 1882. HIS REMOVAL FROM THE SECRETARIAT.

In its obituary notice *The Times* refers to the circumstances under which Mr. Hume left the Secretariat of the Government of India in 1879; and it is there stated that his removal was caused by a conflict with a member of the Government, in which he was "in the wrong." No particulars are given as to the merits of this conflict, which was the turning point in Mr. Hume's official career. In a memoir it is important to clear up a matter of this sort; and fortunately among Mr. Hume's private papers I have found letters and extracts which throw much light on this episode, and show that a cardinal principle, affecting the duties of his office, was involved in what Mr. Hume has called his summary ejection from the Secretariat. To those unacquainted with the working of the bureaucratic system in India, it may not be apparent how severe was the blow thus inflicted. But it must be borne in mind how extraordinarily influential and desirable is the position of a Secretary to Government, who is presumed to be an expert in his own department, who has the first say in all matters coming before the Executive Government, and who has constant access to the Viceroy. He is thus part and parcel of the Supreme Executive, which determines policy, and gives orders from the cool heights of Simla to the rank and file of the service in the plains below. Now what were the reasons given for Mr. Hume's expulsion from this official paradise? The only reason that I find in the papers is contained in a letter from Lord Lytton's Private Secretary of 17 June 1879, where it is stated that the decision "was based entirely on the consideration of what was most desirable in the interests of the public service." This platitude was in reply to a letter from Mr. Hume inquiring in respectful terms the reasons for his removal. No dereliction of duty, or incapacity, was alleged or suggested; the reply was in substance a refusal to give any reason whatever for action altogether out of accord with official precedent. But if no reasons were forthcoming from the Viceroy and his advisers, public opinion, through the Press, was not slow to give its view of the merits. It was clear that a great principle affecting the *morale* of the public service was at stake, and I have before me extracts from leading Anglo-Indian journals, not usually too friendly to Mr. Hume, which declare, in uncompromising terms, that his offence was that he was too honest and too independent. The *Pioneer* characterized the whole proceeding as "the grossest jobbery ever perpetrated"; the *Indian Daily News* said it was "a great wrong"; and the *Statesman*, "Undoubtedly he has been treated shamefully and cruelly." But the best statement of the case is contained in an article in the *Englishman* of 27th June 1879, a part of which I will now reproduce. It is believed to have been from the pen of a distinguished member of the legal profession, and friends of Mr. Hume will be glad to read this vindication of his personal action, and of the principles for which he suffered. Referring to the "measure by which Mr. Hume was summarily superseded and degraded," the *Englishman* writes: "The plea advanced in justification of this arbitrary act was that Mr. Hume habitually, in his minutes on measures coming up for discussion in his department, expressed his views with great freedom, without regard to what might be the wishes or intentions of his superiors. If he believed a particular policy to be wrong, he opposed it without hesitation, using plain language for the expression of his views. We cannot find that any other charge has been brought against him.

He is notoriously a very hard worker, and Government will not easily find his equal in knowledge of the special subjects dealt with in his department. But he is what, according to the present 'Imperial' phraseology, is called insubordinate; this is the alleged ground of his transfer, and this is the point which to us appears most seriously to call for consideration. By 'insubordinate' the Government appears to mean, not that an officer refuses to obey orders, not even that he neglects to carry out in the best possible way orders which he does not himself approve, but that he refuses to join in the cry of 'Peace, Peace' when Government says it is peace, but when it is really war. The present theory of official subordination is, that an officer is not merely to obey orders, not only to do his best to facilitate their execution, but that he is even in his most confidential, semi-official utterances, to suppress any indication of his dissent from what he disapproves, if he knows or has reason to suppose that the Viceroy desires to carry the point. In the days of Lord Dalhousie, Lord Canning, and Lord Mayo, the freest expression of the honest opinions of Secretaries and Under-Secretaries was not only permitted but invited. To have expressed to any one without the charmed circle of the Government opinions adverse to the Government policy, would even then have been considered unpardonable, but inside the circle every official was not only permitted, but required, to express his opinions freely." The article goes on to say that under Lord Northbrook a change was initiated; he could not endure the criticism by his own subordinates of measures he approved; and Lord Lytton intensified this repression: "Clearly there is no security or safety now for officers in Government employment; neither length of service, nor known ability, nor industry, nor all those merits which go to make up a public servant's claims—can avail to protect any man from summary dismissal from any appointment if he either ventures to think for himself, or fails to ingratiate himself with the reigning favourite."

In a close service like that of India, the temptation to cultivate the good graces of those in high office is only too great. Brilliant official prizes, carrying with them large incomes, extensive influence, and pleasant surroundings, await the happy man whom a Viceroy delights to honour. No exceptional discipline therefore is needed to promote the desire for self-advancement. On the other hand a whole service will be demoralized by a policy which penalizes honest independence, and stimulates, instead of checking, mean and selfish ambitions. As regards average human nature, Edmund Burke said in a similar connection, "Men will not look to Acts of Parliament, to regulations, to declarations, to votes, to resolutions. No, they are not such fools. They will ask, What is the road to power, credit, wealth, and honours? They will ask, What conduct ends in neglect, disgrace, poverty, exile?—These will teach them the course which they are to follow. It is your distribution of these that will give the character and tone to your government. All the rest is miserable grimace."

It will be for the public to decide whether, as suggested by *The Times*, Mr. Hume was "in the wrong" when he sacrificed a noble career in the public service rather than accept a policy which must prevent men of rigid principles and unselfish candour becoming the responsible advisers of Governors, Viceroys, and Secretaries of State.

# Allan Octavian Hume

### "The Pope of Ornithology."

It will be convenient here to notice Mr. Hume's work as an Ornithologist; for his transfer in 1879 from Simla to the Revenue Board at Allahabad, not only closed a brilliant official career, but also dealt a disastrous blow to his scientific studies and explorations. In a letter among his private papers, he thus describes the lamentable situation: "In view to working out the Ornithology of the British Empire in Asia I have, during the last fifteen years, spent about £20,000 in accumulating an ornithological museum and library, now the largest in the world, where Asiatic birds are concerned. To form this museum, and to collect data for the proper utilization of the materials thus accumulated, I have had for many years large exploring parties at work in the more inaccessible provinces of the Empire, and have myself, on the rare occasions when the exigencies of the public service have permitted me to take leave, joined in these explorations. The results of all this labour and heavy expenditure are in Simla. To move them is utterly out of the question. I have bequeathed them to the Indian Government on the sole condition of their undertaking the cost of their removal. My transfer to the North-West Provinces removes me permanently for the rest of my service from the vicinity of my museum, debars me from continuing to watch over its progress and utilize as they come in, by recording them in my ornithological journal ('*Stray Feathers*'), as I have done hitherto, the results of the explorations my parties are continually making." In addition to these definite losses to science, Mr. Hume's departure from Simla involved the temporary suspension of his great work on the "Game Birds of India," upon which he had already expended £4,000; also the publication of the scientific results of the

Yarkand expedition, which he was editing, had to be abandoned. It may be added that, in order to accommodate his Ornithological Museum, he had spent £15,000 on Rothney Castle, his beautiful house at Simla. In the following narrative, Colonel C. H. T. Marshall, of the Indian Army, himself a high authority on Ornithology, and collaborator in the "Game Birds of India," bears witness to the supreme importance of Mr. Hume's work in this branch of natural science:

"Allan Octavian Hume was beyond all doubt the greatest authority on the ornithology of the Indian Empire. He, as it were, succeeded Dr. Jerdon, who brought out an excellent book on the Indian avifauna some fifty odd years ago. From the time he began to take an interest in bird life in the early 'sixties he never spared himself, intellectually, physically, or financially, in his endeavours to accumulate material for the great work, 'The Birds of the Indian Empire,' which it was his ambition to give to the world. All his spare time, when free from his official duties, was devoted to forwarding this object.

"For many years he was Commissioner of Inland Customs (known as the Salt Department) in the days when the great Salt Hedge lay across India. This was guarded by a large staff of officials to collect the tax on the salt which was taken through the various gates. Many of these, both English and Indian, became his active and useful helpers. His inspection duties took him all over India. Wherever he went he made a point of endeavouring to obtain recruits and of persuading people he met to interest themselves in ornithology. With his usual generosity he was always ready to help those who could not afford to collect. The result was that he had more than fifty willing helpers between Cape Comorin and Peshawar and from Nepal to Gujarat, as well as in all parts of Burma. One thing he insisted on was absolute accuracy. Every bird-skin had to have a ticket attached showing sex, colouring of soft parts, certain measurements, locality and date of shooting. No egg was added to his collection unless species, place, and date were recorded on the shell. In most cases one of the parent birds was sent also, so as to make sure of the identity of the eggs.

"He endeared himself to all who worked for him. His enthusiasm was infectious and his knowledge of his favourite subject marvellous. He was known familiarly among his fellow-workers as 'The Pope of Ornithology.' In his beautiful Simla home, Rothney Castle, there was a museum for the collection, which was the 'Mecca' for all of us who collected for him; and none of us ever left his hospitable roof and his charming society without having learnt something new on the subject we were studying from our guide, philosopher, and friend.

"The notes on bird life, sent from all parts of India and worked up by himself, grew rapidly and filled many folios. The collection gathered together during some five-and-twenty years amounted to the enormous number of sixty-three thousand bird-skins and nineteen thousand eggs. Everything promised well for the production of one of the finest works on ornithology that could be brought out. But, alas! this great work which was so near completion was never to appear!

"During the winter of 1884, when Simla was under snow and Mr. Hume was down on the plains, his house was left in charge of some of his Indian servants. The precious and voluminous manuscripts were deposited in one of the museum rooms. When he returned in the spring he found to his horror that these invaluable and irreplaceable papers had been stolen and must have been destroyed. Nothing could be done, for there was no clue as to when the theft had been committed. It is supposed that it must have been the dastardly act of a discontented servant. It was a truly crushing blow: the colossal work of over a quarter of a century thrown away! The dream of his life had, as it were, vanished. There was nothing to be done. No hope was left that he would ever reap the reward he had laboured for many years to gain. The great book could never be completed. There was nothing left for him to do but give up the task.

"Few knew how deeply he felt having to come to this decision, for he said but little. The presence of his vast collection only served to constantly remind him of all he had lost; he therefore determined regretfully to part with it. I believe he could have sold it for ten thousand pounds (less really than it was worth) to go to the United States. But he would not dream of selling it or allowing it to go anywhere but to his native land. In 1885 he made a truly noble gift of the eighty-two thousand birds and eggs (all in perfect condition and comprising two hundred and fifty types of newly discovered species) to the British Museum of Natural History in Cromwell Road. The princely offering was gratefully accepted for the nation. It was considered of such importance by the authorities that Dr. Bowdler Sharp, head of the Ornithological Department, was deputed to go to Simla, take it over, and bring it to London. All students of Indian ornithology bless the name of Hume when they go to work in the Museum.

"In 1872 he started at his own expense in Calcutta an ornithological quarterly journal, which he happily named '*Stray Feathers.*' He personally edited it, and articles of great interest from his facile pen graced every issue. It proved to be most useful and popular, and was carried on up till 1899, when he gave it up as he was then living in England, and there was no one else to continue it. In

1873 he published a very excellent book, 'Nests and Eggs of Indian Birds,' a standard work for all interested in ornithology. A revised edition (bringing it up to date) was brought out by Mr. Eugene Oates (a leading authority on the birds of Burma) in 1889–90.

"In 1879 was published that splendidly illustrated work, 'The Game Birds of India,' in three volumes, with one hundred and forty-four coloured plates. Of this Mr. Allan Hume and Captain C. H. T. Marshall were the joint authors. But to Hume must be given the most praise for this book, seeing that a great number of the articles on the different species were from his pen. It was a book greatly needed by sportsmen, and its advent was hailed with delight. The only drawback was that, owing to the heavy cost of production, the edition was limited to one thousand copies. The result is that now it is almost impossible to obtain a copy.

"It was a great loss to ornithology when Hume gave up that science in despair. He has left behind him a name that will always be revered by students of the Indian avifauna. To divert his thoughts from the past and to occupy his time he took up horticulture with the same earnestness and thoroughness as he showed over ornithology. He erected large conservatories in the grounds of Rothney Castle, filled them with the choicest flowers, and engaged English gardeners to help him in the work. From this, on returning to England, he went on to scientific botany. But this, as Kipling says, is another story, and must be left to another pen."

In addition to this noble gift to the nation, Mr. Hume gave to the Natural History branch of the British Museum his unique collection of the heads and horns of Indian big game animals. Part of the collection was presented in 1891, and part bequeathed by will. On the 1st of November 1912 *The Times*, in the following terms, expressed its appreciation of this "unrivalled series of specimens":

"Taken in conjunction with his gift in 1891, of the bulk of his collection of similar objects, it constitutes one of the most valuable acquisitions of the kind ever received by that institution. Apart from the collection presented at various times during the first half of the last century by Mr. Brian Hodgson, the Museum before 1891 was poor in specimens of Indian big game, whereas it now possesses, thanks to Mr. Hume, a collection of these objects which is certainly unsurpassed and probably unrivalled. When Mr. Hume gave the bulk of his collection to the Museum in 1891, he reserved for himself a certain number of picked specimens, and it is these that have now become the property of the nation.

"The collection, which embraces specimens not only from India proper, but from the Himalaya, Kuen-Lun, Pamirs, Burma, etc., was made at a time when the big game of many parts of this area was more abundant than is the case at the present day, and consequently includes finer examples of many species than are now obtainable. And it is this which constitutes its chief value and interest, as it would nowadays be quite impossible to bring together a similar collection. Mr. Hume never did things by halves, and when his collections of big game trophies and birds were made he had collectors or agents at work in all the countries accessible from India.

"Nowadays, it is almost superfluous to mention, sportsmen attach a high value to heads which are 'records,' or nearly such, in the matter of horn-length; and it is quite obvious that as many specimens as possible of this class—as being the finest and handsomest of their kind—ought to be in the national collection. In specimens of this nature the Hume bequest is particularly rich, containing at least five which appear to be 'records' in their particular species, and many others which approximate more or less closely in dimensions to this standard.

"To particularize such specimens on the present occasion would be out of place, more especially as their dimensions are given in Mr. Rowland Ward's 'Records of Big Game.' It must accordingly suffice to state that among the species represented by unusually fine heads are the magnificent wild yak of Tibet, the chiru antelope, with its long V-shaped black horns, of the same area, the Mongolian, Yarkand, and Indian gazelles, the blackbuck of the plains of India, whose spiral horns are, perhaps, the most graceful of all Asiatic ruminants, the markhor goat and ibex of the Himalaya, the so-called ibex of the Nilgiris—which survives only as the result of special Government protection—the lordly gaur, or bison, as it is miscalled by sportsmen, of the Pachmarhi and other Indian hill-ranges, and the great buffalo of Assam. Of the latter animal, it may be mentioned, the Museum has long possessed the 'record' horns (and a wonderful 'record' at that), which were discovered during the eighteenth century in the cellar of a house in Wapping, and presented to Sir Hans Sloane, whose collections formed the nucleus of the British Museum. Wild sheep, too, are strongly represented, the chief species being the massive-horned Tibetan race of the argali, Marco Polo's sheep of the Pamir, whose horns, although less massive, form a longer and more open spiral, the smaller urial of the Punjab and Ladak, and the Tibetan bharal, which stands midway between sheep and goats.

"All the above belong to what naturalists call the hollow-horned ruminants, or those which alone carry true horns; but the collection likewise includes some magnificent heads of deer, whose branching cranial appendages are properly designated antlers. Among these the place of honour belongs to the great so-called Sikhim stag, or shou, of which there are two magnificent heads, one being the actual record. Till Mr. Hume made his collection shou heads were very rare in Europe, and even now they are much thought of even in the neighbourhood of their own country, as is evident from the fact that a skin was presented by the Nepalese Government to the King during His Majesty's tour in India. Other species in the collection include the sambar, the chital, or spotted deer, and the barasingh of the plains of India, the thamin of Burma, remarkable for the unique form of its antlers, and the Yarkand stag, of which specimens have been unobtainable since the Chinese occupation of the country.

"To mount this unrivalled series of specimens adequately will, no doubt, be a matter of time, but when thus mounted and exhibited to the public they will form a magnificent display and a worthy monument to their former owner, by whose munificence the Indian collection of the Museum has been so signally enriched."

## His Retirement in 1882.

In a recent issue of *The Pioneer*, there has appeared a letter signed A. T. B., which are the initials of Captain Beynon, an esteemed friend of Mr. Hume, and a supporter of the Congress. In this letter it is stated, from personal knowledge, that Lord Lytton at one time during his viceroyalty, offered Mr. Hume the Lieutenant-Governorship of the Punjab, but Mr. Hume declined the appointment, saying that the Lieutenant-Governorship meant a great deal of entertaining, and for this neither his wife nor he himself cared: he would much rather be Home Member. Lord Lytton then recommended him for Home Member and a K.C.S.I., but this recommendation Lord Salisbury refused, on the ground that Mr. Hume was "stiffening Lord Northbrook" against the repeal of the cotton duties.

Had Mr. Hume accepted the Lieutenant-Governorship, we should have had a unique example of a one-man administration in full sympathy with the people. The people of his Province would have largely benefited. But it was well for the future of India that, at this critical time, he was set free from the absorbing labours of the supreme executive, and brought into the closest touch with the new forces which the world-spirit was generating among the Indian people.

## THE INDIAN NATIONAL CONGRESS.

It was in 1882 that Mr. Hume retired from the public service; and we now approach the great work of his life—the national movement, of which the Indian National Congress was the political side. As he explained, the Congress organization was "only one outcome of the labours of a body of cultured men, mostly Indians, who bound themselves together to labour silently for the good of India." The fundamental objects of this national movement were threefold, and were recorded in the following terms: First, the fusion into one national whole of all the different elements that constitute the population of India; second, the gradual regeneration along all lines, spiritual, moral, social, and political, of the nation thus evolved; and third, the consolidation of the union between England and India, by securing the modification of such of its conditions as may be unjust or injurious. This, in simple language, sets forth his great scheme for restoring the ancient grandeur of India, in happy partnership with the British people. It was a labour of Hercules, but he brought to the task the necessary elements of genius—the power to formulate a lofty ideal, with infinite patience and industry to work out the practical details ; also he possessed in himself the personality necessary for success in a heroic enterprise. In him we see the true Aryan breed ; of the Western type, in character and *physique* ; with the Norse strain that belongs to Scotsmen dwelling by the North Sea : fair and blue-eyed, stalwart and active, a dauntless lover of freedom. He had within him the compelling spirit of the Berserker ; but his craving was not for battle, but for peace and goodwill. He was thus in full brotherly accord with the Aryan of the East, the meditative and saintly type ; and it pained his very soul that West should deny to East the joys of freedom, which should be the common heritage of both.

In Japan, a peaceful revolution converted a mediæval military despotism into a constitutional government, based on the people's will. By a process of evolution, equally peaceful, the followers of Mr. Hume have set themselves gradually to convert the precarious domination of a foreign bureaucracy into a stable national government, under the ægis of the British Empire. India will then become a tower of strength to the Empire, attached by the strongest ties to this free country, under whose auspices she will, we trust, attain redemption and happiness.

Inspired with these hopes for the future, Mr. Hume became the Founder of the Indian National Congress ; and the foundations were well and truly laid. Trust in the Indian People was the corner-stone ; and the trust was well justified. During twenty-five long and weary years the Congress stood firm ; often under storm and stress : the floods came, and the winds blew upon that house, but it fell not, because it was founded upon a rock. And the labour was not in vain. Writing to Mr. Hume in 1907, Lord Morley said, "I know well your historic place in the evolution of Indian policy." The reforms followed in 1909, and before he passed away the Founder of the Congress was privileged to see the firstfruits of his labours.

A detailed chronicle of these twenty-five years of patient labour would be for political edification, as proving the extraordinary foresight of the Congress leaders in framing their original programme, and their tenacity in following up the claim for a substantial share of popular representation in the government. Such a retrospect would also show the unceasing care with which Mr. Hume, as General Secretary, supervised the widespread mechanism of the organization. But in a brief memoir these particulars cannot be included. I have therefore thought it best to select a few important landmarks in the Congress history, and to deal with them at some length, as best illustrating Mr. Hume's principles and methods of work. Among the most notable of these episodes we may reckon the following : i. The early steps taken in 1883 to form a national organization on a sound constitutional basis ; ii. The first session of the Indian National Congress in 1885 ; iii. The aggressive propaganda addressed to the Indian masses in 1888 ; iv. Mr. Hume's correspondence with Sir Auckland Colvin in the same year ; and v. The propaganda in England. The official recognition of the Congress began with Lord Lansdowne's pronouncement in December 1890, declaring that, as a political organization, the Congress was "perfectly legitimate" ; and was finally confirmed by Lord Hardinge's ceremonial reception of the Congress Deputation in December 1910.

# Allan Octavian Hume

## I. *The Early Steps taken in 1883 to form a National Organization.*

Towards the close of Lord Lytton's viceroyalty, that is, about 1878 and 1879, Mr. Hume became convinced that some definite action was called for to counteract the growing unrest. From well-wishers in different parts of the country he received warnings of the danger to the Government, and to the future welfare of India, from the economic sufferings of the masses, and the alienation of the intellectuals. But happily the arrival of Lord Ripon revived hope among the people, and produced a lull; and Mr. Hume postponed definite organization until, by his retirement from the service, he should be free to act, and able to take advantage of the growing improvement in the popular feeling produced by Lord Ripon's benign presence. Accordingly, the first movement towards a definite scheme is to be found in a circular letter dated 1st March 1883, addressed to the "Graduates of the Calcutta University." The letter opens with these wise and kindly words: "Constituting, as you do, a large body of the most highly educated Indians, you should, in the natural order of things, constitute also the most important source of all mental, moral, social, and political progress in India. Whether in the individual or the nation, all vital progress must spring from within, and it is to you, her most cultured and enlightened minds, her most favoured sons, that your country must look for the initiative. In vain may aliens, like myself, love India and her children, as well as the most loving of these; in vain may they, for her and their good, give time and trouble, money and thought; in vain may they struggle and sacrifice; they may assist with advice and suggestions; they may place their experience, abilities, and knowledge at the disposal of the workers, but they lack the essential of nationality, and the real work must ever be done by the people of the country themselves." Scattered individuals, however capable and however well meaning, are powerless singly. What is needed is union, organization, and well-defined lines of action; and to secure these an association is required, armed and organized with unusual care, having for its object to promote the mental, moral, social, and political regeneration of the people of India: "Our little army must be *sui generis* in discipline and equipment, and the question simply is, how many of you will prove to possess, in addition to your high scholastic attainments, the unselfishness, moral courage, self-control, and active spirit of benevolence essential in all who should enlist." And then he proposed that a commencement should be made with a body of fifty "founders," to be the mustard-seed of future growth; "if only fifty men, good and true, can be found to join as founders, the thing can be established, and the further development will be comparatively easy." The details of the organization would have to be decided by the members themselves. But he made suggestions as to the personnel, discipline, and working methods of the association; and specially he insisted on its constitution being democratic, and free from personal ambitions: the head should merely be the chief servant, and his council assistant servants. This is the principle followed in later years by Mr. Gokhale in his Servants of India Society; and it conforms to the precept, "He that is greatest among you, let him be your servant." And this long letter ends with an appeal, which both stirs and stings: "As I said before, you are the salt of the land. And if amongst even you, the élite, fifty men cannot be found with sufficient power of self-sacrifice, sufficient love for and pride in their country, sufficient genuine and unselfish heartfelt patriotism to take the initiative, and if needs be, devote the rest of their lives to the Cause—then there is no hope for India. Her sons must and will remain mere humble and helpless instruments in the hands of foreign rulers, for 'they would be free, *themselves* must strike the blow.' And if even the leaders of thought are all either such poor creatures, or so selfishly wedded to personal concerns, that they dare not or will not strike a blow for their country's sake, then justly and rightly are they kept down and trampled on, for they deserve nothing better. Every nation secures precisely as good a government as it merits. If you, the picked men, the most highly educated of the nation, cannot, scorning personal ease and selfish objects, make a resolute struggle to secure greater freedom for yourselves and your country, a more impartial administration, a larger share in the management of your own affairs, then we your friends are wrong, and our adversaries right; then are Lord Ripon's noble aspirations for your good fruitless and visionary; then, at present, at any rate, all hopes of progress are at an end, and India truly neither lacks nor deserves any better government than she now enjoys. Only, if this be so, let us hear no more fractious, peevish complaints that you are kept in leading strings, and treated like children, for you will have proved yourselves such. *Men* know how to act. Let there be no more complaints of Englishmen being preferred to you in all important offices, for if you lack that public spirit, that highest form of altruistic devotion that leads men to subordinate private ease to the public weal, that true patriotism that has made Englishmen what they are,—then rightly are these preferred to you, and rightly and inevitably have they become your rulers. And rulers and taskmasters they must continue, let the yoke gall your shoulders never so sorely, until you realize and stand prepared to act upon the eternal truth that, whether in the case of individuals or nations, self-sacrifice and unselfishness are the only unfailing guides to freedom and happiness."

This appeal—from one trusted and beloved by the Indian people—was not made in vain. The men required as founders to initiate the movement, were forthcoming from all parts of India ; and the "Indian National Union" was formed. It was arranged that a Conference should be held at Poona, to enable "all those most interested in this Union to exchange opinions and authoritatively adopt an organization that, in the main, shall approve itself to all." In the meantime a Preliminary Report was issued to members, containing suggestions and conclusions, "the result of the discussion of the subject with all the most eminent and earnest politicians of this Empire." In the first place it is stated that "the Union, so far as it has been constituted, appears to be absolutely unanimous in insisting that unswerving loyalty to the British Crown, shall be the key note of the institution. The Union is prepared when necessary to oppose, by all constitutional methods, all authorities, high or low, here or in England, whose acts or omissions are opposed to those principles of the government of India laid down from time to time by the British Parliament, and endorsed by the British Sovereign, but it holds the continued affiliation of India to Great Britain, at any rate for a period far exceeding the range of any practical political forecast, to be *absolutely essential* to the interests of our own National Development." Amongst the qualifications for membership most commonly insisted on are the following: (1) An unblemished record, public and private ; (2) an earnest and unwavering desire to improve the status, either material, mental, moral or political of the People of India ; (3) marked natural intelligence, adequately developed by education ; (4) a willingness to sink, when occasion demands this sacrifice, selfish and personal, in altruistic and public considerations; and (5) independence of character, coupled with sobriety of judgment. Progress had been made in forming local Select Committees, at Kurrachee, Ahmedabad, Surat, Bombay, Poona, Madras, Calcutta, Benares, Allahabad, Lucknow, Agra, and Lahore, all of whom had promised to attend the Conference at Poona, either as a whole, or in the person of delegates selected among themselves. And it was proposed that until the formation of a Central Committee, there should be a "General Secretary to the whole Union whose duty it should be, not only to visit personally all the Select Committees from time to time and communicate to them the experiences of the other Select Committees, but also to look after the practical details connected with the Conferences, receive all communications from the several Committees and circulate these to others, and generally supervise the office work of the Union." Naturally, the discharge of these toilsome duties fell to the lot of Mr. Hume himself.

Having thus laid the foundations of a national organization, to voice the aspirations of the Indian people, Mr. Hume proceeded to England, in order to consult with friends there, as to the best means of getting a hearing for these aspirations from the British Parliament and Public. His first visit was to Sir James Caird, at Cassencary in Galloway, and there Mr. John Bright met him, having arranged to do so at considerable personal inconvenience. After prolonged consultation with these wise and faithful friends of India, Mr. Hume went on to Lord Ripon at Studley Royal. Thence he proceeded to Lord Dalhousie at Brechin Castle, Mr. Baxter M.P. at Dundee, Mr. R. T. Reid M.P. at Arrochar, Mr. Slagg M.P. at Manchester, and other influential friends. The result of these interviews was reported to his Indian correspondents in an interesting series of letters, written during September 1885. The first matter for consideration was the supply of Indian news to the British Press. The general public in England rarely read more about India than what is contained in the Reuter telegrams which appear in *The Times* and other leading papers; and it had been long the complaint in India that these telegrams have an Anglo-Indian official colouring, and do not do justice to the Indian view of current events and discussions; on the contrary they usually present any case of an Indian complaint in terms hostile to Indian wishes. No opportunity existed for correcting misstatements thus published in England; and the question had assumed additional importance on account of the approaching Conference at Poona, as it was essential that this national organization should not be presented to the British public in an unfair light. Accordingly before leaving Bombay, Mr. Hume arranged for an "Indian Telegraph Union," which was to provide funds to send telegrams on important matters to such leading journals in England and Scotland as would agree to publish them. Mr. Hume undertook to negotiate this matter with the Editors of leading journals, and he later reported that among Provincial papers the following had agreed to receive and publish the Indian Union telegrams: The *Manchester Guardian*, the *Manchester Examiner*, the *Leeds Mercury*, the *Scotsman*, the *Glasgow Daily Mail*, the *Dundee Advertiser*, the *Western Times*, and the *Bradford Observer*. Unfortunately this useful agency was allowed to drop from want of funds. The next question was, how to influence the British public, and especially Members of Parliament? On this question all friends were agreed that at the pending General Election, no hearing could be got for detailed Indian grievances. But it was thought that the opportunity might be taken to obtain from candidates a promise to give attention to Indian affairs. This was the shrewd advice given by Mr. Reid, M.P. (now Lord Loreburn), in a letter addressed to Mr. Hume: "I would recommend you," he said, "to secure two or three men, as influential as you can, in as many constituencies as you can, and get them to write to the candidate, exacting no pledge as to the course of policy but a simple pledge to give attention to Indian affairs, and publish the correspondence in the local papers. Every candidate in the three kingdoms would pledge himself to so easy an obligation. One in ten would keep the pledge and thus give a nucleus of listeners in an Indian debate. The publication of the correspondence would make them afraid wholly to neglect business they had so publicly engaged to consider." The resources at the disposal of the informal Committee in England were not sufficient to carry out so large a scheme, but it may be noted that a limited pledge such as Mr. Reid proposed, was the basis of the Indian Parliamentary Committee, which afterwards did good work for many years in the House of Commons. In the same letter Mr. Reid gives Mr. Hume practical advice on two other points, as to coaching British members on Indian subjects; and as to getting a seat for an Indian in the House of Commons: "You must have coadjutors in Parliament. If you have a few men like yourself busy in England they will find friends inside the House. For there is a real desire in this country to act justly and generously as regards India. But members know nothing. You must have men of honour to inform them of facts. So many impostors and self-seekers are always ready to catch an M.P. to ventilate their grievances, that members are afraid to trust the information given them, and never act on it (if they respect themselves) unless convinced of the integrity of their informants. Therefore you require high-class men to 'coach' and inform members. If they appear and are in earnest, you will get plenty of help." For preference, members would listen to a trustworthy Indian; and if you "succeeded in obtaining a seat for him simply to represent Indian grievances, he would be listened to in the House and would be a real power for good." Besides these definite suggestions, all British friends were agreed that if the cause of India was to make progress among the British people, a vigorous and sustained propaganda must be kept up throughout the country, by means of public meetings, lectures, pamphlets, articles and correspondence in the Press, and by securing the sympathy of local associations and of influential public men. A local British Committee, to act as the guiding and propelling power in this work, was evidently required; but it was felt that the time had not yet come to reorganize on a permanent basis the informal Committee of sympathizers, who were then attending to Indian interests in England.

II. *The First Session of the Indian National Congress.*

Having accomplished his mission in England, and established touch with the leading progressives there, Mr. Hume returned to India, in order to watch over the arrangements for the first Conference of the Indian National Union, which had been fixed to be held at Poona from the 25th to the 30th of December 1885. The Poona Reception Committee had made admirable preparations. To accommodate the delegates, the Poona Sarvajanik Sabha (the leading Association of the Deccan) granted the use of the Peshwa's palace of Heerabagh, which with its gardens, stands beautifully situated upon the lake under the temples of Parbati Hill. Further it was decided that, looking to the national importance of the movement, and the wide support it had received in all parts of India, the Conference should formally assume the title of the Indian National Congress. Unfortunately, a few days before the time fixed for the assemblage, several cases of cholera occurred in Poona; and it was considered prudent to transfer the meeting to Bombay. Thanks to the exertions of the Bombay Presidency Association, and the liberality of the managers of the Goculdas Tejpal Sanscrit College and Boarding House (who placed the grand buildings above the Gowalia Tank at the Association's disposal), everything was ready by the morning of the 27th of December 1885, the date when the representatives began to arrive. Thus it happened that Bombay had the honour of holding the first session of the "Indian National Congress," while Calcutta provided, as the first President, Mr. W. C. Bonnerjee—the wise head and firm hand, that took the helm when the good ship was launched.

Now looking back at the proceedings of this first Congress, we must be struck by the success which, though long delayed, ultimately attended the definite claim which formed the core of the resolutions, viz., the prayer for substantial popular representation on the Indian Legislative Councils. It will be well to reproduce in full this memorable resolution, which (a good augury) was moved by the Hon. K. T. Telang C.I.E., seconded by the Hon. S. Subramania Iyer, and supported by the Hon. Dadabhai Naoroji. It was No. 3 on the Congress programme, and ran as follows: "Resolved.—That this Congress considers the reform and expansion of the Supreme and existing Local Legislative Councils, by the admission of a considerable proportion of elected members (and the creation of similar Councils for the North-West Provinces and Oudh, and also for the Punjab) essential; and holds that all Budgets should be referred to those Councils for consideration, their members being moreover empowered to interpellate the Executive in regard to all branches of the administration; and that a Standing Committee of the House of Commons should be constituted to receive and consider any formal protest that may be recorded by majorities of such Councils against the exercise by the Executive of the power which would be vested in it, of over-ruling the decisions of such majorities." This is the resolution of which Mr. Hume said that it "indicated the very essence of the great task which the people of India, at last a nation, one and indivisible henceforth and for ever, was soberly and deliberately girding up their loins to undertake." The struggle lasted long; and ultimately this prayer for popular representation was granted by Lord Morley's reforms of 1909. But what a world of misunderstanding and suffering, of affections alienated and passions aroused, of secret conspiracy, and outrage, and Russian methods of repression, might have been avoided if the Administration had been wise in time, and listened long ago to the counsels respectfully tendered by a friendly and law-abiding people!

But here it must be noted that, although the Congress movement has always been looked on with undisguised hostility by that section of officials who are in permanent antagonism to the educated and independent classes, this disfavour has not, as a rule, extended to the higher authorities. This was especially the case at the outset. Indeed, in initiating the national movement, Mr. Hume took counsel with the Viceroy, Lord Dufferin; and whereas he was himself disposed to begin his reform propaganda on the social side, it was apparently by Lord

Dufferin's advice that he took up the work of political organization, as the matter first to be dealt with. Lord Dufferin seems to have told him that as head of the Government he had found the greatest difficulty in ascertaining the real wishes of the people; and that, for purposes of administration, it would be a public benefit if there existed some responsible organization, through which the Government might be kept informed regarding the best Indian public opinion. He further observed that, owing to the wide differences in caste, race, and religion, social reform in India required local treatment, rather than the guidance of a national organization. These kindly counsels were received with grateful appreciation by all concerned. Indeed so cordial were the relations, that Lord Dufferin was approached with a view to the first Congress being held under the presidency of Lord Reay, then Governor of Bombay. Lord Dufferin welcomed the proposal, as showing the desire of the Congress to work in complete harmony with the Government, but he considered that many difficulties would be involved if a high official presided over such an assembly. The idea was therefore abandoned, but none the less the first Congress was opened with the friendly sympathy of the highest authorities.

### III. *Aggressive Propaganda in India of 1888.*

At the second Congress, which was held at Calcutta, Lord Dufferin showed his sympathy by inviting the members of the Congress, as "distinguished visitors," to a garden party at Government House. And a similar compliment was paid to them by Lord Connemara, the Governor of Madras, in the following year. But after that there came a change. For years were passing on, and there were as yet no signs of any concessions being granted. To the ardent mind of Mr. Hume platonic expressions of sympathy by the authorities were a mockery while nothing practical was being done; for he was obsessed by the misery of the masses, and the belief that most of it was preventible. Intimately acquainted with the inner life of the Indian village, and a witness of successive famines with all their horrors, he was familiar with the sorrows of the impoverished peasantry, and in a pamphlet entitled "The Old Man's Hope," he thus made impassioned appeal to the comfortable classes in England: "Ah men! well fed and happy! Do you at all realize the dull misery of these countless myriads? From their births to their deaths, how many rays of sunshine think you chequer their gloom-shrouded paths? Toil, toil, toil; hunger, hunger, hunger; sickness, suffering, sorrow; these, alas! alas! are the key notes of their short and sad existences." The special travail of his soul was for these suffering masses, and his prayer was, "God save the people"; echoing the cry of Ebenezer Elliott, the Corn-Law poet:

"When wilt Thou save the People?
Oh God of Mercy—when?
The People, Lord—the People!
Not thrones and crowns, but men.

"Flowers of thy heart, Oh God, are they.
Let them not pass like weeds away,
Their heritage a sunless day.
God save the People!"

With such feelings, and his heart hot within him, it was not in the nature of the man to wait with calmness when nothing was being done. The pool of Bethesda had been stirred, but no healing had followed. Time was passing; the patient was in danger of collapse; but there were no signs of a remedy; and Mr. Hume felt that at all hazards the authorities must be awakened to the urgency of the case. In no grudging spirit he acknowledged the benefits conferred by British rule: the blessings of peace, and protection to life and property. But the *Pax Britannica* has not solved the economic problem, nor availed to preserve the debt-laden and despairing peasantry from the ravages of famine and disease. British rulers, he maintained, had failed, not from any lack of good intention, but from insufficient knowledge. The sufferings of the Indian masses from famine and disease arose from poverty; and this poverty was preventible, if the Government would take into their counsels experienced representatives of the people, who know exactly where the shoe pinches. But the Government would take no action. What was to be done? The case was one of extreme urgency, for the deaths by famine and pestilence were counted, not by tens of thousands, or by hundreds of thousands, but by millions; and in order to constrain the Government to move, the leaders of the Indian people must adopt measures of exceptional vigour, following the drastic methods pursued in England by Bright and Cobden in their great campaign on behalf of the people's food.

In the days of his youth Mr. Hume had witnessed the progress of this campaign, and he told how the delegates of the Corn-Law-League were refused a hearing by the House of Commons; and then Cobden, in few but weighty words, announced the new propaganda, which was to have such far-reaching results for the people of England: "The delegates," he said, "have offered to instruct the House; the House has refused to be instructed; and the most unexceptionable and effectual way will be by instructing the nation." "So," continued Mr. Hume, "has it fared with us; our educated men singly, our Press far and wide, our representatives at the

National Congress—one and all—have endeavoured to instruct the Government, but the Government, like all autocratic governments, has refused to be instructed, and it will now be for us to instruct the nations, the great English nation in its island home, and the far greater nation of this vast continent, so that every Indian that breathes upon the sacred soil of this our Motherland may become our comrade and coadjutor, our supporter, and, if needs be, our soldier in the great war that we, like Cobden and his noble band, will wage for justice, for our liberties and rights."

In pursuance of such a propaganda in India, Mr. Hume set to work with his wonted energy, appealing for funds to all classes of the Indian community, distributing tracts, leaflets, and pamphlets, sending out lecturers, and calling meetings both in large towns and in country districts. Throughout the country over 1,000 meetings were thus held, at many of which over 5,000 persons were present; and arrangements were made for the distribution of half a million of pamphlets; translations into twelve Indian languages being circulated of two remarkable pamphlets, entitled "A Congress Catechism," by Mr. Veraraghava Chariar of Madras, and "A Conversation between Moulvi Furreeduddeen and one Rambuksh of Kambakhtpur," showing by a parable the necessary evils of absentee State landlordism, however benevolent the intention may be.

It will naturally be asked, What was the attitude of the Indian Government, not constitutionally tolerant of popular agitation, towards this bold and drastic political propaganda? The Hon. Mr. Gokhale, speaking at the Hume Memorial Meeting in London on the 6th of August last, indicated the probable inclinations of the Government under such circumstances. "No Indian," he said, "could have started the Indian National Congress.

Apart from the fact that any one putting his hand out to such a gigantic task had need to have Mr. Hume's commanding and magnetic personality, even if an Indian had possessed such a personality and had come forward to start such a movement embracing all India, the officials in India would not have allowed the movement to come into existence. If the founder of the Congress had not been a great Englishman and a distinguished ex-official, such was the official distrust of political agitation in those days that the authorities would have at once found some way or other to suppress the movement." This conclusion was no doubt correct; and it is certain that, from the time when the propaganda was addressed to the masses, the official attitude, which till then had been one of more or less friendly neutrality, became distinctly antagonistic. Mr. Hume himself realized this, and said, "Friends come with solemn faces and say in grave voices: You mean well, but you are stirring up feelings, you are exciting passions, the issues of which you cannot foresee; you are letting loose forces that you cannot control." And he took occasion to explain his position, and put forward his Apologia, in a speech at a great meeting at Allahabad on the 30th of April 1888, which was published under the title of "A Speech on the Indian National Congress, its Origin, Aims, and Objects." Speaking of the spirit which it was desired to inculcate among the people, he quoted what had been placed on record at the inception of the Congress, "since this record embodies, not merely the ideas of one or two men, but the harmonized views of a very large number of the ablest, best, and most advanced thinkers of the nation." The record declares that the Congress was intended "to foster a wider altruism and a more genuine public spirit, by concentrating the most strenuous efforts on great national problems, and diminishing the absorption in local or purely selfish interests—to educate all who took part in it, not merely in the arts of public speaking and debate, developing the faculty of thinking out clearly opinions, and expressing them lucidly to others, not merely in habits of accuracy and research, but also in the practice of self-control, moderation and willingness to give and take—to educate them in fact into what has been described as a genuine Parliamentary frame of mind—to familiarize the country with the methods and working of representative institutions on a large scale, and thus, as this familiarity grew, to demonstrate to the Government and people of England that India was already ripe for some measure of those institutions to which the entire intelligence of the country so earnestly aspires."

Having thus made clear what was the inner spirit of the movement, he proceeded to show that there was no cause for fearing political danger from Congress teaching: "The people are taught to recognize the many benefits that they owe to British rule, as also the fact that on the peaceful continuance of that rule depend all hopes for the peace and prosperity of the country. They are taught that the many hardships and disabilities of which they complain are after all, though real enough, small in comparison with the blessings they enjoy, but that all these grievances may be and will be redressed if they all join to press their views and wishes unanimously, but temperately, on the Government here and on the Government and people of England. The sin of illegal or anarchical proceedings is brought home to them, and the conviction is engendered that by united, patient, constitutional agitation they are certain ultimately to obtain all they can reasonably or justly ask for, while by any recourse to hasty or violent action they must inevitably ruin their cause and entail endless misery on themselves." And then, in eloquent words, he pleaded for a logical continuity, on the part of the British nation, of the humane and enlightened educational policy of 1833 and 1854: "It is the British Government in their noble enthusiasm for the emancipation of this great people—God's trust to them—from the fetters of ignorance, who by the broadcast dissemination of Western education and Western ideas of liberty, the rights of subjects, public spirit and patriotism, have let loose forces which, unless wisely guided and controlled, might, nay sooner or later certainly must, involve consequences which are too disastrous to contemplate. And it is precisely to limit and control these forces and direct them, while there is yet time, into channels along which they can flow auspiciously, bearing safely the argosies of progress and prosperity on their heaving waves, that this Congress movement was designed. The Government has, broadly speaking, never realized the vast proportions of the coming flood which is being engendered by the noble policy of which in 1833 Lord Macaulay was so prominent an exponent; and it is we of the Congress, who through good repute and ill repute, careless what men say of us if only haply God may bless our efforts, who standing between the country and the coming development, are labouring—labouring almost frantically—to provide in time channels through which this surging tide may flow, not to ravage and destroy but to fertilize and regenerate."

### IV. *Correspondence with Sir Auckland Colvin.*

The Allahabad speech, boldly justifying a propaganda addressed to the masses, on the model of the Anti-Corn-Law League, was certainly successful in compelling the serious attention of the authorities. But the new departure, and especially the campaign in the rural districts, had also the effect of causing some genuine alarm among the officials. I do not wish to enlarge upon the proceedings of the more excitable and high-handed functionaries, who put their trust in espionage; who stimulated among Mahomedans a class hostility to the movement; who desired to suppress the Congress; and who recommended that Mr. Hume should be deported. This was only a passing official phase, not countenanced by the highest authorities, which we may well forget. But it is altogether different in the case of a critic of the position and abilities of Sir Auckland Colvin, and in order to judge regarding the merits, or demerits, of this new and active propaganda, we cannot do better than study the letters which, in October 1888, passed between Sir Auckland Colvin and Mr. Hume, and which were published, with Sir Auckland's consent, as a pamphlet, under the title of "Audi Alteram Partem." Sir Auckland Colvin was a very distinguished member of the Civil Service; he held the high office of Lieutenant-Governor of the North-West Provinces; he claimed to belong to the "Liberal Official Camp"; and, until the new departure which followed the third Congress, held at Madras, he was distinctly friendly to the Congress movement. The grounds therefore of his disapproval, which are stated in calm and courteous language, are deserving of the most respectful consideration. His letter also was welcome at the time it was written, because it gave Mr. Hume a favourable opportunity of publicly making his position clear, and replying in detail to the objections raised by a competent and responsible critic. So important indeed is this correspondence, that I would gladly have reproduced the letters *in extenso*, but they are too detailed and (in parts) too technical for this brief memoir, Sir Auckland Colvin's letter extending to over twenty printed pages, and Mr. Hume's to nearly sixty; but I will give ample extracts from the text, with a summary of the arguments on both sides.

Looking to these considerations, Sir Auckland's letter of remonstrance, and Mr. Hume's answer, vindicating his action, may be taken as the pleadings in the Congress case at the most critical period of the movement; showing what could be said for and against the bold and drastic policy of appealing to the masses of the Indian people, on the lines marked out and followed in England by Bright and Cobden. Sir Auckland considered that this new departure was premature and dangerous; on the other hand Mr. Hume held that it was the path of safety, and the only way of averting national disaster.

Upon this issue Sir Auckland's argument may be summarized as follows. The question, he said, was one of both principle and methods. As regards principle and the general objects of the Congress, he was more or less in sympathy; especially he was in favour of the expansion of the Legislative Councils. And as regards methods, he saw little to object to in the earlier proceedings of the Congress, as manifested at Bombay and Calcutta in the sessions of 1885 and 1886. But his sympathy received a "severe check" after the Madras Congress of 1887, when the propaganda became aggressive, on the model of the Anti-Corn-Law campaign in England. He considered that in the existing political condition of India such a propaganda was premature, and likely to defeat the objects in view. He further anticipated definite mischief from this aggressive or denunciatory method, because it tended to excite hatred of the Government and the officials, and because agitation would produce counter-agitation, dividing the country into strongly hostile camps. He objected to the tone and substance of the pamphlets recently issued, which in his opinion misrepresented the policy and action of the Government; and, commenting on the attitude of the Congress, he considered that its supporters unfairly claimed to represent the Indian population. Finally, he suggested that the reformers should occupy themselves with social reform, as being more needed than political reform, for the welfare of the people.

These objections are no doubt serious. But at the same time it was reassuring that they were directed against the methods, and not against the principles or objects of the Congress. As to these, Sir Auckland Colvin, keen observer and careful administrator as he was, saw little to disapprove. On the contrary, he expressed sympathy with the leading proposal of the Congress programme—the expansion of the Legislative Councils on a popular basis—which was designed to bring the most able and trustworthy Indian intellectuals into co-operation with the Government, in the grand task of rescuing the millions of India from the miseries of ignorance, of destitution, and disease. Such doctrine was in accordance with common sense. It needed no justification; and its practical wisdom was proved by the logic of events. For the early leaders of the Congress—men like Mr. Dadabhai Naoroji, Mr. Justice Ranade, Sir Pherozesha Mehta, Mr. W. C. Bonnerjee, Mr. Justice Budrudin Tyabji, Mr. Surendranath Banerjea, Mr. Bhupendranath Básu, Mr. Gokhale, and Mr. Krishna Swami Iyer—became the trusted advisers of the Government; and, by force of merit, rose to the highest offices, whether judicial, municipal, legislative, or executive. There is no truer saying than, that in the affairs of life, as in mechanics, where there is no resistance there is no support; and it was not long before the Government realized the value of strong and independent men, who afterwards proved to be the firmest support of ordered progress, in the dark times of trouble and unrest.

So much for the principles and objects; there remains to consider the experiences of Congress methods. On this part of the question Mr. Hume lost no time in replying to Sir Auckland Colvin's challenge. The main point of his defence was that, so far from the action of the Congress being premature, the fear was that it might be too late. But before dealing with this central question, it will be convenient to say a few words regarding the minor objections raised. With regard to the charge that the Congress pamphlets excited hatred to the Government, Mr. Hume replied that nothing was to be gained by ignoring the notorious practical grievances felt by the peasantry. Every one who makes himself acquainted with the village life knows how bitter, when they talk among themselves, are the complaints, not loud but deep, with regard to the costly and unsuitable civil courts, the corrupt and oppressive police, the rigid revenue system, the galling administration of the Arms Act and the Forest Act. What is wanted is justice, cheap, sure, and speedy; a police that the people can look up to as friends and protectors; a land revenue system more elastic and sympathetic; a less harsh administration of the Arms and Forest laws. Accordingly the policy followed in the pamphlets and lectures has been, not to "blink or pretend to ignore the grave evils that exist." In every hamlet there are the natural leaders of the people who "acknowledge and are grateful for the many unquestionably fine things we have done for them." But they "equally recognize and grumble over the many bad things they have to put up with by reason of our well-intentioned ignorance of how to fit our burden properly to their backs." Therefore "in our pamphlets we approach these intelligent men with sympathy, we admit their grievances, but we put them in a milder shape than they themselves do; we tell them that 'the English Government is superior to all other governments in the world, for its fundamental principle is to shape its policy according to the wishes of the people.' We tell them emphatically that it is not the individual governors or officials who are to blame for the shortcomings of the administration, but the system, the form of that administration; and we further show them how, by loyal and constitutional efforts, they can secure the amelioration of that system, and a remedy for many of the evils they have to contend against." This is the answer to the charge of exciting hatred against the Government and the officials.

Next, as to the risk of a counter-agitation, dividing the country into two hostile camps. On this point it is not now necessary to recall the personal incidents of the opposition to the Congress raised by Sir Syed Ahmed and his friends. Mr. Hume considered that this opposition was not important, and he held that, excluding an inappreciable fraction, the whole culture and intelligence of the country was favourable to the Congress. And he dealt somewhat severely with the anti-Congress party, which he said was made up of a small knot of Anglo-Indians, mostly officials, supported by a section of the Anglo-Indian Press; "a few Indian fossils, honest, but wanting in understanding; a few men who in their hearts hate British rule, or are secretly in the employ of England's enemies"; and a certain number of "time-servers, men not really in their hearts opposed to the Congress, but who have taken up the work of opposition to it, because it has seemed to them that this will 'pay.'" Further he maintained that the Congress, instead of dividing, was uniting, was binding in harmonious co-operation, men who previously scarcely met except to quarrel and even to fight; and he instanced the case of Salem, till recently a hot-bed of religious antagonism between Hindus and Mahomedans.

Mr. Hume highly appreciated the distinctive characteristics of the Moslems—their manly energy and democratic instincts; and he did not believe that the opposition represented their genuine feeling. According to his view the hostile stimulus came from the outside, from a few ill-advised officials who clung to the pestilent doctrine of "Divide et impera," and from unfriends of the Government, who hated a movement which sought to unite all parties and all creeds in friendly co-operation under the ægis of the British Empire. He therefore denounced the counter-agitation as artificial and mischievous. Further, he held that, more than any other community, the Mahomedans would benefit by the united action which would bring them into the current of modern progress; he trusted to their good sense to realize this; and he believed that within three years the anti-Congress party would collapse. We have reason to hope that eventually opposition to the Congress will cease. At the same time it appears that there was some foundation for the apprehension suggested by Sir Auckland Colvin; and that the active Congress propaganda did stir up, to a certain extent, religious rivalries which had, more or less, become dormant. The reason for this was twofold. In the first place the Hindus, as regards numbers, were predominant in the Congress. This was because the Congress was mainly supported by the English-speaking class, and it was the Hindus who had most readily accepted Western education. In the second place, the Mahomedans, who mostly conducted their education on the old lines, had fallen behind in the learned professions and in the competition for the public service. It was therefore not unnatural that a section of them regarded the Congress with suspicion and jealousy, as an instrument of aggrandizement for the Hindus. It cannot be said that this feeling has died out even at the present day, but happily it is not generally shared by the rising generation of educated Mahomedans, nor by leaders like His Highness the Aga Khan. For his part, Mr. Hume indignantly repudiated the idea that the Mahomedans could not hold their own in fair competition. "The wretched plea," he said, "about the Mahomedans being so inferior to Hindus that they will have no chance if a fair field is conceded to all classes and sects, is monstrous. I swear that no good true Mahomedan ever, if he reflected on it, would put forward so base a libel on his coreligionists. Haven't I had thousands of both under my own eye? Have I not hundreds of Mahomedan friends?" He then named Sir Salar Jung, Mr. Justice Budrudin Tyabji, Mr. Justice Syed Mahmud and other distinguished public men; and continuing, he said, "The whole thing is a shameful libel on the Mussulmans, who, alike in times past and present, have ever held and ever will hold their own, and whatever advantages flow from an improved and gradually developing administration of India, believe me that the Mussulmans will ever obtain, in virtue of their hereditary capacity, energy, and pluck, a full and fair share." To this he added a personal note, saying, "I speak warmly on this subject, because even inferentially to charge me with participation in any scheme injurious to the best interests of the Mussulmans, to whom in the past I have owed so much, amongst whom I have still so many friends, is an insult. Can I forget the brave friends and followers who in those dark days of danger and distress stood by me, protected me, and fought for and beside me in 1857—aye, and in too many cases sealed with their lifeblood the record of their friendship and fidelity? NEVER!"

Sound education is what is wanted to enable the Musselmans to do justice to themselves. And to provide this, their leaders at the present day have been working, both by their scheme for a Moslem University, and by supporting Mr. Gokhale's Bill in the Viceroy's Council for free and compulsory elementary education. May they prosper in their patriotic labours; and find encouragement from the sympathy of so trusty a friend as Mr. Hume, and from his warm expression of regard and gratitude!

It is not necessary to go at any length into other minor points raised by Sir A. Colvin. With regard to his objection, that the Congress had no right to claim to be representative of the people of India, Mr. Hume pointed out that in Great Britain the Mother of Parliaments represented directly only a small fraction of the people, and that less than 10 per cent. of the population took part in the parliamentary elections, even in such advanced constituencies as the City and County of Aberdeen. He might also, without unfairness, have referred to the doings of the Free and Independent electors of Weymouth, who not so long ago had sent to the Imperial Parliament two "representatives" of the English people. He claimed that the Congress represented the culture and intelligence of the country, a claim which was afterwards confirmed, in part at least, by Lord Lansdowne, when he said that the Congress represented "the more advanced Liberal party." As regards the suggestion that the Congress should devote itself to social in preference to political reform, Mr. Hume referred to the declared objects of the great movement of which the Congress formed only a part. The movement sought the regeneration of India on all lines, spiritual, moral, social, and political. The Congress was directed to national and political objects desired by all classes in

India. On the other hand social requirements varied according to race, caste, and creed, so that they had to be dealt with by separate organizations; but, as a general rule, it was found that the workers for political progress were the most active friends of social reform.

We have now to consider the main contention between Sir Auckland Colvin and Mr. Hume. Sir Auckland considered the propaganda premature and mischievous; Mr. Hume considered it necessary for the safety of the State. Which was right? To those unfamiliar with Indian affairs, it may seem strange that there should be this acute difference of opinion between two experienced officers, both members of the same service, both sympathetic with Indian progress, both keenly anxious for the public welfare. But the interpretation is simple, and is well understood by every Indian. The difference of opinion is an irreconcilable one, depending on the point of view, whether of the ruler or the ruled. For after his retirement from the service in 1882 Mr. Hume had identified himself with the Indian people, living among them as one of themselves. The difference therefore between the Lieutenant-Governor and the Congress leader, was the difference of the view held by the British administrator judging his own work, and that of the Indian subject with personal experience of its defects. Mr. Hume tells his friend how he may learn the truth: I can clearly see, he says, that you "still look upon our government through the rose-tinted official spectacles that so long obscured my sight. But leave the service, become a nobody, mix freely with the people, hear what they have to say when not afraid to speak their minds, study the reverse of the shield, and, knowing you as I do, I know well that you would wholly change your views." The one way of learning the truth is, as Mr. Hume says, to "mix freely with the people"—the people of all classes, from the highest to the lowest; prove to them that you are trustworthy, and they will trust you and tell you all the truth. This is not only the best way, but the only way. For whatever information English officials as foreigners, can acquire is, and must be, obtained from the people themselves; and it may be obtained from the right men, or from the wrong men. And in this matter the ordinary official is under great disadvantages, because as the local magnate and the dispenser of official favours, he is naturally surrounded by self-seekers, who do not deal in disagreeable truths. It is the interest of these men to flatter him, and, for their own protection, to keep him out of touch with the independent men of his district; also to persuade him that these men are unfriendly and even (vague and terrible word) "seditious." Many an official is thus brought into antagonism with the best men, and falls into the hands of the secret police, and the miserable class of spies and informers. Independent Indians of high character and public spirit are to be found in every province, and in every district; but they must be sought out with care; they do not willingly present themselves in official quarters, where they may be met with suspicion from the authorities, and insult from underlings. Now it was this class of high-minded men, in solid agreement throughout India, friends of India and England, whom Mr. Hume took as his advisers. They saw the danger looming ahead, "tremendous in the immediate future," from the misery of the masses, acted on by the bitter resentment of individuals among the educated class; and they warned him that early action must be taken if disaster was to be averted. Accordingly, in answer to Sir Auckland, Mr. Hume admitted that there was a certain risk in the Congress agitation, that the experiment was quite new in India; and that circumstances were not wholly favourable; also he explained that, had it been possible, he personally would gladly have postponed the propaganda for some years. "But," he wrote, "no choice was left to those who gave the primary impetus to the movement. The ferment, the product of Western ideas, education, inventions and appliances, was at work with a rapidly increasing intensity, and it became of paramount importance to find for its products an overt and constitutional channel for discharge, instead of leaving them to fester, as they had already commenced to do, beneath the surface. I have always admitted that in certain Provinces and from certain points of view the movement was premature, but from the most vital point of view, the future maintenance of the integrity of the British Empire, the real question when the Congress started was, *not*, is it premature, but is it too late—will the country *now* accept it? . . . A safety-valve for the escape of great and growing forces, generated by our own action, was urgently needed, and no more efficacious safety-valve than our Congress movement could possibly be devised." In this matter Mr. Hume, to use his own phrase, was "in deadly earnest." Appreciating the nature of the Indian people, their conservative instincts, their law-abiding character, their astonishing endurance and docility, unless driven out of their ancient quietude by feelings of despair, he felt confident that he was following the right and safe course in showing them how hope could be maintained, and that there was a peaceful and orderly line of conduct by which relief from their sufferings might be obtained.

As a lesson to the people of this country in world politics, the teaching of Mr. Hume in this matter is of the first importance, showing where the real danger in India lies—the danger under the surface, arising from material suffering among the masses and resentment among the irreconcilable section of the dissatisfied intellectuals. The danger is enhanced by the fact that the autocratic power is exercised by a handful of foreigners, alien to the population in language, race, and creed, and belonging to a masterful nation singularly regardless of the feelings and prejudices of others. Consequently the mutterings of the storm are unheeded by them, and great disasters, like the Mutiny of 1857, and the tragedies of Cabul, come upon them like a bolt from the blue. To listen therefore to the warnings of "the man who knows," like Mr. Hume, is vital to the continuance of British rule in India. History tells a similar story. It is true that in Venice oligarchic government lasted for a long term of years, but there the dominion over the people was exercised by men of their own race, men of singular political insight, who kept themselves well-informed, and dealt skilfully with the beginnings of trouble. Such favourable conditions are not enjoyed by the Indian bureaucracy. As pointed out by Mr. Hume, the true historic parallel is to be found in the regime of the Bourbons at the close of the eighteenth century: they had neither eyes to see nor ears to hear, and sudden destruction was brought upon them by the hatred of the intellectuals energizing the dull despair of the peasant masses. No doubt when the crisis comes, the Englishman meets disaster in a fine spirit, and usually comes out more or less victorious in the end. But there is a grievous waste of life and labour involved in this purblind trust in the sad method of "muddling through."

### *Indian Religious Devotees.*

Looking to Mr. Hume's experiences in the Mutiny of 1857, as briefly described in these pages, and the boldness and resource which he displayed, no one can doubt the importance which attaches to his personal belief in the reality of the threatened danger. Also his judgment was confirmed by that of a wide circle of Congress friends spread over the different Provinces. But in addition to this, information and warning came to him from a very special source, that is, from the leaders among those devoted, in all parts of India, to a religious life. Among his papers there exists a very illuminating memorandum regarding "the legions of secret quasi-religious orders, with, literally, their millions of members, which form so important a factor in the Indian problem." As regards those professing to be religious devotees, he recognizes that a large proportion of the Faquirs, Bairágis, and Sádhus are little better than rogues and impostors. But if there is dross, there is also gold; and among the heads or *Gurus* of these sects are to be found men of the highest quality who, like the ancient Hebrew prophets, have purged themselves from earthly desires, and fixed their aspirations on the highest good. These religious leaders, through their *Chelas* or disciples, are fully informed of all that goes on under the surface, and their influence is great in forming public opinion. It was with these men that Mr. Hume came into touch, towards the end of Lord Lytton's viceroyalty. The ground of sympathy may have been in part religious, for Mr. Hume was a keen student of Eastern religions. But the practical reason why these men made a move towards him was because they feared that the ominous "unrest" throughout the country, which pervaded even the lowest strata of the population, would lead to some terrible outbreak, destructive to India's future, unless men like him, who had access to the Government, could do something to remove the general feeling of despair, and thus avert a catastrophe. "The jungle is all dry," they said; "fire does spread wonderfully in such when the right wind blows, and it is blowing now, and hard." "This," writes Mr. Hume, "is how the case was put to me, and knowing the country and the people as I do—having been through something of the same kind, though on a small scale, in the Mutiny—and having convinced myself that the evidence of the then existing state of the proletariat was real and trustworthy, I could not then and do not now entertain a shadow of a doubt that we were then truly in extreme danger of a most terrible revolution."

What the nature of this evidence was, cannot be better told than in his own words: "The evidence that convinced me, at the time (about fifteen months, I think, before Lord Lytton left) that we were in imminent danger of a terrible outbreak was this. I was shown seven large volumes (corresponding to a certain mode of dividing the country, excluding Burmah, Assam, and some minor tracts) containing a vast number of entries; English abstracts or translations—longer or shorter—of vernacular reports or communications of one kind or another, all arranged according to districts (not identical with ours), sub-districts, sub-divisions, and the cities, towns, and villages included in these. The number of these entries was enormous; there were said, at the time, to be communications from over thirty thousand different reporters. I did not count them, they seemed countless; but in regard to the towns and villages of one district of the North-West Provinces with which I possess a peculiarly intimate acquaintance—a troublesome part of the country no doubt—there were nearly three hundred entries, a good number of which I could partially verify, as to the names of the people, etc." No doubt the district here referred to was Etawah, where he had been chief executive officer for many years. He mentions that he had the volumes in his possession only for about a week; into six of them he only dipped; but he closely examined one covering the greater portion of the North-West Provinces, Oudh, Behar, parts of Bundelcund and parts of the Panjab; and as far as possible verified the entries referring to those districts with which he had special personal acquaintance. Many of the entries reported conversations between men of the lowest classes, "all going to show that these poor men were pervaded with a sense of the hopelessness of the existing state of affairs; that they were convinced that they would starve and starve and die, and that they wanted to do *something*. . . . They were going to do *something* and stand by each other, and that something meant violence," for innumerable entries referred to the secretion of old swords, spears, and matchlocks, which would be ready when required. It was not supposed that the immediate result, in its initial stages, would be a revolt against our Government, or a revolt at all, in the proper sense of the word. What was predicted was a sudden violent outbreak of sporadic crimes, murders of obnoxious persons, robbery of bankers, looting of bazaars. "In the existing state of the lowest half-starving classes, it was considered that the first few crimes would be the signal for hundreds of similar ones, and for a general development of lawlessness, paralysing the authorities and the respectable classes. It was considered certain also, that everywhere the small bands would begin to coalesce into larger ones, like drops of water on a leaf; that all the bad characters in the country would join, and that very soon after the bands attained formidable proportions, a certain small number of the educated classes, at the time desperately, perhaps unreasonably, bitter against Government would join the movement, assume here and there the lead, give the outbreak cohesion, and direct it as a national revolt."

Such were the specific warnings addressed to Mr. Hume. The forecast of trouble throughout India was in exact accordance with what actually occurred, under my own observation, in the Bombay Presidency, in connection with the Agrarian rising known as the Deccan Riots. These began with sporadic gang robberies and attacks on the moneylenders, until the bands of dacoits, combining together, became too strong for the police; and the whole military force at Poona, horse, foot, and artillery, had to take the field against them. Roaming through the jungle tracts of the Western Ghauts, these bands dispersed in the presence of military force, only to reunite immediately at some convenient point; and from the hill stations of Mahableshwar and Matheran we could at night see the light of their camp fires in all directions. A leader from the more instructed class was found, calling himself Sivaji the Second, who addressed challenges to the Government, offered a reward of Rs. 500 for the head of H.E. Sir Richard Temple (then Governor of Bombay), and claimed to lead a national revolt upon the lines on which the Mahratta power had originally been founded.

Before quitting this subject one special point must be noticed, viz., Mr. Hume's belief that the reports in the seven volumes must necessarily be true, because they were the reports of *Chelas* to their *Gurus*. This point is important on the merits of the case; and it is also relevant to the present memoir, because it illustrates the bent of his mind, which induced him to study with eager interest the peculiar phases of Eastern religious thought. His explanation is as follows: "A *Chela* is a son, pupil, apprentice and disciple, all in one, and a great deal more. None of these terms give any adequate conception of the sanctity of the tie between *Chela* and *Guru*. No man becomes a true *Chela* who has not given up all worldly objects and finally determined to devote all his efforts, and concentrate all his hopes, in what *faute de mieux,* I may call, spiritual development. All *Chelas* are bound by vows and conditions, over and above those of ordinary initiates of low grade. No *Chela* would, I may almost say *can* deceive his *Guru,* in whom centre all his hopes of advancement; no teacher will take on the *Chela* cast off by another. What a real *Chela* says to his *Guru* you may accept as the absolute truth, so far as the speaker is concerned. He may be mistaken, he cannot lie." Apparently some of the reporters, from being *Chelas* in their earlier years, had afterwards returned to ordinary secular life: "Many were respectable worldly men (a few of whom, in my part of the country, I actually knew), but these were all men who had gone through some initiations, and taken binding vows in earlier life, though from one cause or another they had given up the path. But the majority, I was told, were devotees, men of every sect and creed in the country, all initiates in some of the many branches of the secret knowledge, and all bound by vows, they *can* not practically break, to some farther advanced seeker than themselves, who again must obey others, and so on, until you come to the leaders who are of *no* sect and *no* religion, but of *all* sects and *all* religions." He further explains that absolute secrecy is an essential feature in the life of these devotees; and this accounts for the fact that ordinarily even the existence of these religious sects is unknown to the best informed Europeans, and to the majority of the educated Indians themselves. It was only under the stress of peculiar circumstances, and to avert calamity, that the leaders opened communications with Mr. Hume, although he always refused to come under their special pledges. His attitude of co-operation was thus defined: "I have promised always to do what I am asked, when the thing to be done involves, so far as I can judge, no moral wrong, and never to give out, without permission, anything I have been informed of or shown, unless it should appear to me a distinct moral duty not to hold my tongue."

### V. *The Propaganda in England.*

We have now to shift the scene from East to West. For the great scheme to which Mr. Hume had set his hand consisted, as regards its political side, of two parts, each complete in itself, neither effective without the other. There was essential work to be done in India; and there was essential work to be done in England. In India, a programme of reforms was being matured; in England, that programme had to be pressed on the attention of Parliament and the public. For Mr. Hume was firmly convinced that the British people desired fair play for India, and would see that justice was done, provided only they understood the merits of the case. No doubt the original connection of England with India was purely self-seeking. But gradually there came an awakening of the national conscience, and the sentiment of duty in the performance of a national trust. India, therefore, helpless in official bonds, should make known her grievances to her big brother, the all-controlling Demos of the British Isles; but in order to obtain relief, it was necessary that she should raise her voice in tones loud enough to rouse the friendly but slumberous giant.

These were the views held by Mr. Hume; and he called on Indian reformers to make a strenuous effort to induce the British public to shake off the torpor of an ignorant optimism, and to restore the continuity with the best traditions of British statesmanship, as declared by such leaders as Edmund Burke, Lord Macaulay, and John Bright: the policy embodied in the wise Statute of 1833, and the noble Proclamation of Queen Victoria in 1858.

It will be remembered that in 1885, the first year of the Congress, Mr. Hume paid a visit to this country, and in consultation with Parliamentary friends, sketched out a plan of campaign for the propaganda in England. We have now to see what action was taken in this direction. At first he cherished the hope that some concessions might, by the force of persuasion, be obtained in India from the Viceroy in Council, but when year after year passed away without any response to the Congress prayer, he became convinced that no reform of any value could be expected from the official hierarchy at Simla, and that it was from England that the impulse must come, if any satisfaction was to be obtained for Indian aspirations. Accordingly in a letter, dated 10th February 1889 from Calcutta, he pressed upon Congress workers the vital need for the British propaganda on an adequate scale. He pointed out that in India the work of the Congress in consolidating public opinion had been in great measure accomplished, and that, broadly speaking, all Indian progressives were agreed as to the proper remedies for Indian grievances and disabilities, but "our European officials—who are here all-powerful—in consequence of service traditions and bureaucratic bias, as a body deny utterly the justice of our contentions, and are not to be convinced by anything that *we* can ever possibly say. We impute no blame to them for this—it is only natural—for the tendency of all the reforms we advocate is to curtail the virtually autocratic powers now exercised by these officials, and unless they were more than human they must necessarily be antagonistic to our programme. Giving all due credit to our European officials, and acknowledging their many merits, nothing nevertheless is more certain than that, so long as we confine our reclamations to their ears, we shall never secure those important reforms that *we* all know to have now become essential, not only to our own welfare but to the auspicious continuance of British rule in India. . . . Our only hope lies in awakening the British public to a sense of the wrongs of our people—to a consciousness of the unwisdom and injustice of the present administration. The least that we could do would be to provide ample funds—for sending and keeping constantly in England deputations of our ablest speakers to plead their country's cause—to enable our British Committee to keep up an unbroken series of public meetings, whereat the true state of affairs in India might be expounded—to flood Great Britain with pamphlets, leaflets, newspapers, and magazine articles—in a word to carry on an agitation there, on the lines and scale of that in virtue of which the Anti-Corn-Law League triumphed." Would that India had followed this wise leadership! A frontal attack on bureaucratic power, firmly entrenched at Simla—with all the armoury of repression at its command—was hopeless. But success was within reach, by means of a flanking movement, that is, by an appeal to the British elector; for the elector's vote gives office to the Prime Minister, and the Prime Minister nominates the Secretary of State, to whom the Viceroy in Council, with all the official hosts, is subordinate. Unfortunately the party of progress in India have never properly realized the practical advantage of this method, and in succeeding years have brought upon themselves endless woes by futile resistance in India to irresistible force, while neglecting to conduct effectively in England the operations which, with a moderate expenditure of labour and of money, would have secured to them a painless victory.

# Allan Octavian Hume

*The British Committee of the Indian National Congress.*

The first steps towards a Congress organization in England were taken in 1887, when Mr. Dadabhai Naoroji, then residing in London, volunteered to act as Agent for the Congress; but he was not supplied with funds, and being engaged in business, he could only spare a small portion of his time, so that practically little was done. But in 1888 an important move forward was made, when Messrs. W. C. Bonnerjee and Eardley Norton joined Mr. Dadabhai in England, and succeeded in enlisting for their cause the great democratic champion, Mr. Charles Bradlaugh M.P. Further, a paid Agency was established under Mr. W. Digby C.I.E.; offices were taken at 25 Craven Street, Strand; and a vigorous campaign was carried out in the country. Ten thousand copies of the Report of the third Congress, and many thousand copies of speeches and pamphlets were printed and circulated; while Messrs. Bonnerjee and Norton, in connection with the Agency, addressed a number of public meetings, and Mr. Bradlaugh delivered many lectures on Indian questions in different parts of England. All this Mr. Bradlaugh did gratuitously, solely in the interests of India, but of course the Agency had to pay for the public halls, advertisements, and other incidental expenses. During the seven months of this work about £1700 were spent. For the current year 1889 the expenditure was estimated at £2500, and this amount Mr. Hume called upon India to provide. Concluding his note, he wrote, "In order first to guide the operations of this Agency, and second to check its accounts and audit them in England before they are sent out to us, a strong Committee of influential gentlemen is now being formed in London. Later I shall be able to report more fully on this matter; at present I am only in a position to say that Sir William Wedderburn, Mr. Dadabhai Naoroji, and Mr. Bradlaugh will certainly be upon it, and that it will include others of the most prominent and trusted of our friends in England."

Action was taken in accordance with the above scheme, and the required Committee was formed on the 27th July 1889. It consisted of Sir W. Wedderburn (chairman), Mr. Dadabhai Naoroji, Mr. W. S. Caine M.P., and Mr. W. S. Bright McLaren M.P., with Mr. W. Digby as secretary, and subsequently the Committee was joined by Mr. John Ellis M.P., Mr. George Yule, Mr. W. C. Bonnerjee, Sir Charles Schwann M.P., Sir Herbert Roberts M.P., Dr. G. B. Clark, and Mr. Martin Wood. The constitution of this Committee was confirmed by a Resolution of the Congress of 1889, and Rs. 45,000 were voted for its maintenance, the amount to be raised by a proportional contribution from each of the Provincial Congress Committees. The title finally adopted was, "The British Committee of the Indian National Congress." In September 1892 Mr. Digby resigned the secretaryship, and the office was removed to Nos. 84 and 85 Palace Chambers, Westminster, a very convenient locality opposite the Houses of Parliament; and these rooms, suitably furnished, the walls hung with portraits of Congress worthies, and with an Indian library contributed by Mr. Dadabhai Naoroji and other friends, became the permanent centre of operations for the Congress propaganda in England.

It has been the practice to elect, as temporary members of the Committee, any leading Congress supporters who happen to be on a visit to England. This brings the Committee into touch with the most recent developments in India, and adds much strength to its position, as will be understood from the list of these temporary members, which has included such names as Sir Pherozeshah Mehta, Mr. Surendranáth Banerjea, Mr. Subramania Iyer, Mr. Mudholkar, Mr. Gokhale, Mr. D. E. Wacha,

Mr. Romesh Dutt, Mr. H. A. Wadia, Mr. H. N. Haridas, Mr. A. Chaudhuri, Mr. M. A. Jinnah, and Mr. Bhupendranáth Básu. On account of his long absences in India, it was not till the 6th of May 1890 that Mr. Hume was himself able to join as a member, and for the first time to attend a meeting of the Committee.

As a Congress leader, and as an early member of the British Committee, Mr. W. C. Bonnerjee stood preeminent, combining wise counsels with steady perseverance and ungrudging liberality. His lamented death occurred on the 21st of July 1906, and Mr. Hume writing of him as "one of the best and truest friends" he ever had, thus described his work for India: "From the very outset, he had thrown in his lot, unhesitatingly, with the Congress movement of which he was one of the originators, and from early in 1885 up to this his lamented decease, he adhered to and supported that movement, alike through good and evil report, giving it all the strength of his high character and position, great abilities and widespread influence. Probably no other Indian gentleman of modern times ever exercised so great an influence over his countrymen at large—not merely in Bengal, but throughout India—as did Mr. W. C. Bonnerjee, who from the first day that he put his hand to the plough of Reform very early in 1885, never grudged his time, his talents or his money, whenever and wherever he saw, or thought he saw, that the cause of India's people might be in any degree aided or promoted by any or all of these."

As time went on, changes occurred in the permanent membership of the Committee. Early colleagues dropped out, and new friends were added. In 1903 there came an important accession of strength when Sir Henry Cotton K.C.S.I. joined the Committee, and from time to time other sympathetic Parliamentarians were added, including Mr. Alfred Webb M.P., Mr. Hart Davies M.P., Mr. C. J. O'Donnell M.P., Dr. Rutherford M.P., Mr. Mackarness M.P., Mr. Philip Morrell M.P., Mr. O'Grady M.P. (as representing the Labour Party), and Mr. A. M. Scott M.P. Some of those who co-operated most actively with the Committee, such as Sir Charles Dilke, and Mr. Samuel Smith, preferred not to join, on the ground that they would be able to work more effectively in the House of Commons for India without being members of an outside Committee.

Now as regards the success of the work undertaken by the British Committee, it must be borne in mind that the chief difficulty in England for those seeking justice to India, arises from the antagonism of the India Office, where the Council of the Secretary of State has always been the stronghold of reactionary officialdom. As Mr. Hume put it, the India Office is "an organization perpetually employed in popularizing the official view of all Indian questions," and if Indian grievances are to be remedied, this hostile influence must be met—in Parliament, on the Platform, and in the Press—by "an organization equally persistent and strenuous in disseminating the people's view of these same questions." This therefore was the task before Mr. Hume and his friends; and they sought to fulfil each of these duties—as regards Parliament, by organizing an Indian Parliamentary Committee; as regards the Platform, by arranging public meetings throughout the country; and as regards the Press, by founding the journal *India* as an organ of Congress views. Each of these enterprizes must here be described a little in detail.

### *The Indian Parliamentary Committee.*

It is in Parliament that vital issues are decided; and as few Indian readers are familiar with the technicalities of Parliamentary methods, it seems necessary to explain the difficulties which an independent member desiring reform has to encounter, and to show how completely, as regards India, official influences are dominant in the House of Commons; also it is important to understand that things have gone from bad to worse since 1858, when the direct administration of India was assumed by the Crown. In theory, the Secretary of State in Council is supposed to be the servant of the House of Commons; and in theory, he is supposed to occupy a position of judicial impartiality, as the Court of Appeal for Indian grievances. But neither of these suppositions has any foundation in fact. In point of fact, no matter which Party is in power, the Secretary of State, as a member of the Government commanding a Parliamentary majority, is not the servant but, in Indian matters, the master of the House of Commons; and in dealing with the independent member who questions authority, he does not even affect impartiality, but comes before the House as the indignant apologist of the Department for which he is responsible. Also, he is free to treat the troublesome member with scant courtesy, because his salary is drawn by himself direct from the Indian Treasury, and no inconvenient motion can be brought forward for a reduction on the estimates. Further, as noted above, the Parliamentary situation has materially deteriorated since the days of the old East India Company, because the House of Commons regarded the Company with a wholesome jealousy, as being a privileged monopoly; and since the privileges were granted for a period of only twenty years, a searching enquiry into the whole system of administration was on each occasion carried out before the charter was renewed. Now this is all changed. The wholesome jealousy is dissipated; and for more than half a century there has been no periodical enquiry, such as was before provided automatically, no account of stewardship, no day of reckoning for official delinquencies. To complete the picture, one more point must be noticed. In other departments of the administration, an independent member seeking redress of grievances, gets ready support from the Front Opposition Bench. But this is not so in the case of a Radical daring to voice India's complaint of destitution, famine, and pestilence. Him a Tory Secretary of State denounces for his malignant, though unaccountable, want of patriotism, while the ex-Minister, emerging from his retirement on the Liberal benches, re-echoes these sentiments, praises his own past administration, and proclaims "the unspeakable blessings of British rule." With a few honourable exceptions, the London Press follows suit, finding subject for amusement when the House empties itself, as soon as it is a question of India's suffering, not seeing any shame in this shameful disregard of national duty.

To stem this tide of official optimism, and get a hearing for India's complaint, is beyond the power of a private member, unless endowed with the personality and authority of a Bright, a Fawcett, or a Bradlaugh. The only hope is in combination; and fortunately in the House of Commons there has never been wanting an element of independence and love of fair play, if only it can be reached and made available. Acting therefore on the lines indicated in Mr. Hume's letter of 5th September 1885 (*v.* p. 55), steps were taken during the Session of 1893 to establish an "Indian Parliamentary Committee," not committed to any particular measures, but pledged to attend to Indian interests, and to see that justice was done. The earlier movements in the same direction are interesting, and may be noted here. Under the name of the "India Reform Society," an organization was founded in 1853, mainly through the exertions of Mr. John Dickinson, for the purpose of promoting combined and well-directed action among the friends of India. At that time the Charter of the East India Company was about to expire, viz., on the 30th of April 1854, and the immediate object of the Society was to secure that the customary enquiry by Parliament, previous to the renewal of the Charter, should be full and impartial. By means of the facts thus collected, and supplied to him through Mr. John Dickinson, Mr. Bright was enabled to make the noble speeches on India, which led to the issue of Queen Victoria's memorable Proclamation in 1858, and did so much to determine the wise and humane policy under Lord Canning, which followed the Indian Mutiny. In 1883 Mr. John Bright approved the formation of an informal Indian Committee, having for its object to secure combined Parliamentary action. Some fifty names were obtained of Members of Parliament, willing to co-operate on the broad ground of a just and sympathetic policy towards India; and it was arranged that out of these an Executive Committee of five or six should be formed. Of this Executive Committee, Mr. Bright consented to act as Chairman. Supported by this Committee, Mr. John Slagg, Senior Member for Manchester, in 1885, moved for a full Parliamentary enquiry into Indian administration. He secured a place for his motion to enquire into the Government of India Act of 1858, and Lord Randolph Churchill agreed to second it. But, unfortunately, a change of Government prevented the motion coming on, and the opportunity was lost.

The Committee of 1883, which has fallen into abeyance, was revived on the 27th of July 1893, when Sir W. Wedderburn and Mr. Caine invited a few leading independent members to dine with them at the House of

Commons, in order to discuss Indian affairs. On that occasion Sir W. Wedderburn, after briefly explaining the situation, moved the following Resolution: "That it is desirable to form an Indian Parliamentary Committee for the purpose of promoting combined and well-directed action among those interested in Indian affairs." This Resolution was seconded by Mr. Caine, supported by Mr. John E. Ellis, and carried unanimously. Mr. Jacob Bright then moved, "That the following members form the Indian Parliamentary Committee, with power to add to their number." The names, which included all those present, were the following: Mr. Jacob Bright, Mr. Caine, Mr. John E. Ellis, Dr. W. A. Hunter, Mr. Illingworth, Sir Wilfrid Lawson, Mr. Walter B. McLaren, Mr. Swift MacNeill, Mr. Dadabhai Naoroji, Mr. Herbert Paul, Sir Joseph Pease, Mr. J. Herbert Roberts, Mr. R. T. Reid, Mr. Samuel Smith, Mr. C. E. Schwann, Mr. Eugene Wason, Mr. Alfred Webb, and Sir W. Wedderburn. This motion was seconded by Mr. Illingworth, and supported by Mr. Samuel Smith, Mr. Dadabhai Naoroji, Mr. Swift MacNeill, and Mr. Schwann, and was carried unanimously. On the motion of Mr. Caine, seconded by Mr. S. Smith, Sir W. Wedderburn was appointed Chairman, and Mr. J. Herbert Roberts Secretary of the Committee. From time to time new members joined, so that at the close of the Session the Indian Parliamentary Committee comprised no fewer than 154 members of the House of Commons, a formidable body from a Parliamentary point of view. From among these the following were elected to form a Working Committee: Mr. W. S. Caine, Mr. J. E. Ellis, Mr. W. S. B. McLaren, Mr. D. Naoroji, Mr. J. G. Swift MacNeill, Mr. Herbert Roberts (Secretary), Mr. C. E. Schwann, Mr. S. Smith, Mr. A. Webb, Sir W. Wedderburn (Chairman), and Mr. H. J. Wilson.

At this time the financial condition of India was very critical. The Viceroy, Lord Lansdowne, described the situation in the following terms: "To leave matters as they are means for the Government of India hopeless financial confusion; . . . for the taxpayers of India the prospect of heavy and unpopular burdens; and for the country as a whole a fatal and stunting arrest of its development." Under these circumstances, a letter (dated 1st July 1894) was addressed, on behalf of the Committee, to Mr. Henry Fowler, then Secretary of State for India, containing a searching criticism of Mr. Westland's Budget; and the subsequent proceedings in the House of Commons, followed by the debate on the Indian Budget, resulted in Mr. Dadabhai Naoroji's motion for a Parliamentary enquiry, which wrung from Mr. Fowler the appointment of the Welby Royal Commission on Indian expenditure and the apportionment of charge between India and the United Kingdom.

At the elections during the ten succeeding years of Tory domination the Indian Parliamentary Committee lost many of its most active members. But at last the wave of reaction spent its force; the tide turned; and at the General Election of January 1906 the Tory Government was wrecked, and power came into the hands of the most democratic Government, and the most democratic House of Commons, that had existed since the Reform Act of 1832. With a House of Commons so favourably constituted, no time was lost in reviving the Indian Parliamentary Committee. At the invitation of Sir W. Wedderburn, a company of Members of Parliament and others interested in Indian affairs, met at breakfast on February 28th 1906, at the Westminster Palace Hotel; and afterwards a Conference was held "with a view to reconstitute the Indian Parliamentary Committee, and generally to consider what action may usefully be taken in the new Parliament to advance the interests of the Indian people." Mr. Leonard Courtney (now Lord Courtney) presided at the Conference, and opened the proceedings; and speeches were made by Mr. Schwann M.P., Mr. J. M. Robertson M.P., Lord Weardale, Mr. Frederic Harrison, Mr. Herbert Roberts M.P., Sir Henry Cotton M.P., Mr. Pickersgill M.P., Mr. J. A. Bright M.P., Mr. H. Nuttall M.P., Mr. C. J. O'Donnell, M.P., Sir George Robertson M.P., Mr. Byles M.P., Mr. Hastings Duncan M.P., Mr. Hume, Mr. Dadabhai Naoroji, and Sir W. Wedderburn. Resolutions in pursuance of the objects of the meeting were passed unanimously; the Indian Parliamentary Committee was duly reconstituted; and eventually nearly two hundred Members of Parliament became members of the Committee.

### *The Journal "India."*

Next as regards propaganda in the Press. Indian reformers should bear in mind that without a recognized organ in the Press no cause has in England any chance of success. Whether the cause is Temperance or Free Trade, Land Reform, Irish Nationalism, or Female Suffrage, all reformers find it indispensable to be well represented in the Press, and spend large sums annually with this object. But as regards India the need is far greater, (1) because the subject of Indian grievances is unfamiliar, and distasteful to the national vanity of "the man in the street"; (2) because in the London Press articles on Indian subjects are mainly supplied by Anglo-Indians unfavourable to Indian aspirations; and (3) because there are no Indian electors to bring pressure upon Parliament and the Government. If India ceases to have an organ in the Press of this country, she will be held to have abandoned her appeal to the British public and the British Parliament. Accordingly, as early as 1890, the British Committee established the journal *India*, to place before the British public the Indian view of Indian affairs. At first the journal was issued at irregular intervals; in 1892 it appeared as a "monthly," being issued on the second Friday of each month; and on the 7th of January 1898 it first appeared as a "weekly" in its present form.

Besides its functions of advocacy, *India* performs an essential duty in supplying trustworthy information to the British public. The British Committee constantly receives requests for accurate information on Indian affairs from Members of Parliament, from journalists, and from lecturers and platform speakers. In order to supply such a demand it is absolutely essential to have a complete and handy record of current facts, events, and opinions. And this is furnished by *India*, which is a store-house from which arms and materials are supplied to all those who are willing to strike a blow on behalf of India. The special correspondent of *The Times*, a none too friendly critic of the Congress, bears witness to the performance of this useful duty, when he says of *India* that "it may not have a very large circulation at home, but is the chief purveyor of Indian news to a large part of the Liberal Press."

Unfortunately there is another side to the question, *i.e.*, the financial side. As already noted, journals in this country which preach reform, whether political or social, can only do so at the expense of their supporters. The advocacy of an altruistic cause, going counter to selfish interests, popular prejudice, and national vanity, cannot be a commercial success: in the school of the world it is the vender of sweets, not the doctor with his "nauseous draught" that is welcome. And this is peculiarly the case with regard to the Congress cause in England. For any hope of success the grievances of India must be forced on the attention of the British public, and this is the duty imposed on the British Committee. Under the circumstances no source of political influence can with safety be neglected. And accordingly, from week to week, by a free distribution of the journal *India* to Members of Parliament, journalists, political associations, clubs, and reading-rooms, the Committee have placed before the British public the case of India, her needs and grievances. But for want of funds this work has been carried out with increasing difficulty. Rigid economy had to be exercised, preventing various desirable developments, and with their scanty resources the Committee could not have obtained the services of editors possessing such exceptional qualifications as Mr. Gordon Hewart and Mr. H. E. A. Cotton, had not these gentlemen been influenced by their warm sympathy with the cause. The matter is of extreme importance, and it will be necessary to urge the Congress to make suitable and permanent provision for its propaganda work in England. This should be done by forming a permanent propaganda fund, and by securing in London the continued presence of responsible Indian exponents of Congress views.

### *Public Meetings, Addresses, and Interviews.*

There remains to be considered what can be effected by public speech and personal persuasion. This work has been done in past years by public meetings and lectures, by addresses to associations and other select audiences, by social entertainments, and by interviews with Ministers, Members of Parliament, editors, and other public men. In this work the best results were obtained when accredited Congress leaders, like Sir Pherozeshah Mehta, Mr. Surendranáth Banerjea, Mr. Gokhale, and Mr. Bhupendranáth Básu came to speak at first hand on behalf of their fellow-countrymen. To show the nature of the work, a brief description may be given of the campaigns carried out by Mr. Gokhale in 1905 and 1906. In 1905 four Delegates from India were expected, and the British Committee arranged for some fifty meetings at important centres all over the country. Only two Delegates, Mr. Gokhale and Mr. Lajpat Rai, were able to come; and much of Mr. Lajpat Rai's time was taken up by a visit to America, where he addressed meetings at New York, Boston, and Chicago. But Mr. Gokhale's campaign in Yorkshire and Lancashire was a brilliant success. His visit to Lancashire, under the auspices of Sir Charles Schwann and Mr. Samuel Smith, was specially opportune, with reference to the Partition of Bengal, and the boycott of Manchester goods. At Manchester he addressed four most important meetings, (1) the Federated Trades Councils, (2) the Manchester Chamber of Commerce, (3) a meeting of merchants connected with Indian trade, and (4) the Manchester Liberal Association. At each of these meetings he made a different speech, in each case specially adapted to the requirements of his audience. The Chairman of the British Committee, who accompanied him, can bear witness to the profound impression produced on his hearers by the accuracy of his information and the cogency of his arguments. Good meetings were also held in London, and he had a gratifying reception by the undergraduates of the "Union" at Cambridge, where his motion in favour of more popular institutions for India was carried by 161 to 62. The Fabian Society also held a special meeting to hear an address from him. At this time a Conservative Government was in power, and gave its support to Lord Curzon's reactionary and repressive policy. Mr. Gokhale's main duty therefore in 1905 was to arouse public opinion in this country by means of the Platform and the Press. In 1906, after presiding at the Benares Congress, he returned to England as the accredited representative of the Congress. But the situation had much changed in the meantime. Our political friends were in power; so that to address public meetings was a secondary matter; and his main object was to come into touch with, and inform, Ministers and Members of Parliament, upon whom the future of India mainly depended. For this purpose he not only addressed meetings of the Indian Parliamentary Committee, but also personally interviewed about 150 members of the House of Commons, and secured from them promises of active interest in Indian affairs. As regards interviews with Ministers, the most important were naturally those he had with Mr. Morley, who accorded to him a series of long interviews, in which he was able to place fully before the newly appointed Secretary of State the needs and aspirations of the Indian people. Mr. Ellis, the Under Secretary for India, who was an original member of the British Committee, also had cordial interviews with Mr. Gokhale, and invited him to a breakfast party, where he and other Parliamentary friends expressed their sympathy. Finally the Prime Minister, Sir Henry Campbell-Bannerman, accorded him an interview, and gave him a most kindly hearing.

### *Support of the Propaganda.*

These particulars of the propaganda in England, as regards Parliament, the Press, and the Platform, have been set forth in some detail for a specific purpose, viz., to impress on the Indian public the very precarious position of Indian interests, and the absolute need of an organization in England, well-informed, vigilant, and with resources sufficient to take effective action whenever a crisis occurs. At present in England the friends of progress are in power. For a time the sea is calm, and the wind is fair. But who can tell how long this will last? Is any one so simple as to suppose that the Imperialistic Party is dead, because for the moment it is "hushed in grim repose"? Owing to the complications of home and foreign affairs, the fate of all Ministries in this country hangs on a thread. Sooner or later there must be a change; and power will come into the hands of those out of sympathy with Indian aspirations. Surely the people of India have not already forgotten what they suffered under the Party of retrogression, of race and class prejudice, of aggression abroad and repression at home! Are they content to await passively the repetition of the same experiences? What the Indian people have to realize is, that *action in favour of Indian aspirations does not spring spontaneously from the ordinary operation of British institutions, but has ever been the result of persistent and laborious personal effort on the part of outside reformers working, both in India and England, on the lines indicated by Mr. Hume.* If from time to time an advance has been achieved, it is due to the sympathy of the British democracy, acting under the propulsion of independent reformers. No reform has ever been initiated by the leaders of the Indian bureaucracy. On the contrary, the class interests which hold the lever of power at Simla and at the India Office, are continuously working to strengthen the official position. Not only have they always done their best to prevent new concessions, but when opportunity has offered, they have taken away the privileges inherited from a former generation of reformers—the liberty of the Press, the right of public meeting, municipal self-government, the independence of the Universities. These ill-starred measures of reaction, combined with Russian methods of police repression, brought India under Lord Lytton within measurable distance of a revolutionary outbreak; and it was only just in time that Mr. Hume and his Indian advisers were inspired to intervene. Through their devoted efforts the gulf between the rulers and the ruled was bridged over by the Congress structure, which bore the strain of Imperialism for seven years under Lord Curzon, and made straight the paths for Lord Morley's reforms of 1909, and the Royal Declarations of 1911. Let any thoughtful Indian reflect what fatal developments, much more serious than sporadic outrages, must have followed from popular despair if, during those years, the controlling influence of the Congress had not existed in India, and if, after the Liberal victory at the polls, a duly authorized statement of grievances, and of needed reforms, had not been systematically pressed upon responsible statesmen in England. From the past learn the future; and let the people of India be assured that disaster will follow, and follow (not undeservedly) from their own default, if effort is relaxed, if the organization in England, built up so painfully, is allowed to go to pieces, and if the results of twenty-five years of labour are thrown away.

### A Proposed Memorial.

We learn from India that influential friends in different parts of the country desire to raise a memorial to Mr. Hume; and it seems very appropriate that such a movement should be initiated, as it has been, in the United Provinces, in which he worked for many years, and where he was so well known and so well beloved. May I venture to make an appeal with regard to the form of the memorial, and to remind his friends of the views expressed by him in a circular letter which he addressed to Congress workers on the 16th of February 1892, regarding a proposed memorial to Pandit Ajudhia Náth? As is well known, there was no one for whom he had a more sincere personal regard than Pandit Ajudhia Náth, but in this letter he wrote, "For God's sake waste no money on memorials or any other minor enterprise; give every farthing you can spare to the general cause." The purpose for which he claimed the money was for propaganda in this country: "Our only hope," he wrote, "lies in awakening the British public to a sense of the wrongs of our people." What then is my suggestion? It is this: Mr. Hume's dearest wish was for the emancipation of India, and he held that this could be secured only by an insistent appeal to the British people. The best memorial therefore to the faithful friend who has now passed away would be an "Allan Hume Memorial Fund," having for its object to perpetuate his work, and prevent the destruction of his dearest hopes.

### "Farewell to India."

In 1894 he bade farewell to India, and on the 18th of March of that year an address expressing affection and gratitude was presented to him by the Bombay Presidency Association, signed with the honoured names of Pherozeshah Mehta, President, and Dinsha Edalji Wacha, N. G. Chandavarkar, and A. M. Dharamsi, Honorary Secretaries. Replying to this address, Mr. Hume gave a forecast of world politics, as affecting India: at that time the forces of militarism and reaction in every country seemed to be gaining strength; in England the party opposed to Indian aspirations would probably come into power; a great European war was possible, with the most disastrous consequences. There were black clouds darkening the horizon; and Mr.

Hume exhorted his hearers to be courageous and steadfast: "Let nothing discourage you," he said, "hold fast to that conviction which all the best and wisest share: that right must, and ever does triumph in the end, and that nations have only to deserve, to secure all that they aspire to. Checks to progress *may* come—alas, I fear, *must* come—as I have warned you, and many years may pass during which apparently you gain no single inch—nay, it may be, even lose ground; but throughout it all work on dauntlessly, preparing for the good time assuredly coming—work on ceaselessly, and India shall one day reap a glorious harvest of your labours. Let nothing—no temporary checks, no temporary losses—dishearten you. The spirit of the age is behind you, and win you must before the end comes. . . . No matter how impossible immediate progress may, owing to the tyranny of circumstances, appear, you are bound as true men to hammer on—hammer, hammer, hammer—never relaxing your efforts, and so gradually acquiring that habit of unwavering persistence that as a nation you so sadly lack. You can work at high pressure for a week, but to run at low pressure, uniformly and unwearyingly for a year, is beyond most of you; and yet this power of sustained continuous exertion is the very first requisite for political success, and if these anticipated checks only teach you this, they will prove not misfortunes but blessings in disguise." If unhappily a great European war broke out, and England was involved, he adjured them to give united and ungrudging support to the British people, who with all their defects were "a noble nation, that has ever sounded the advance to all the listening peoples of the world along the paths of freedom —the nation to which you owe most of what you now most highly prize": they should "rally as one man to the side of those little isles which have been justly designated Freedom's last stronghold—Freedom's keep! Yes, in the nobler sense of the words, a great war will be India's opportunity—opportunity for proving that if in periods of peace she clamours—at times somewhat angrily—for equal civil rights, in the hour of *war* she is ever ready and anxious to accept equal military risks." After this stirring appeal, which was greeted with "prolonged applause," Mr. Hume turned from politics to social admonition, urging his hearers to raise the general level, physical, mental, and moral, of the people, in order that India might become great, and free, and happy. For while, with the boldness of a Hebrew prophet, Mr. Hume rebuked the rulers, no less faithfully did he deliver his message to the people, warning them against the sins which most easily beset them. This he did from a compelling sense of duty, speaking "as a father parting for ever from his children that he loves, and whose future he fears for." "I am an old man," he said, "I have lived my life amongst you, and perhaps know as much of India as a whole as any one living; but for all that I do not pretend to dogmatize—I only tell you what I who love you believe to be essential to your ultimate success." First, he warned them—you must reform your marriage laws; you must prevent the marriage of immature persons; racial degeneracy is the inevitable consequence of such marriages. You must have the sound body for the sound mind: "Herein lies the first foundation-stone of that national greatness which we fondly hope will hereafter clothe, as with a robe of glory, old India and her regenerated sons." Secondly, you must educate the boys of the whole nation—*and also the girls:* "Assuredly there is no greater, grander, or more glorious work before you than the reinstatement of India's women on the exalted pedestal which is their due, and which your wiser forefathers, thousands of years ago, when India was great and glorious, accorded to them." Finally, with reluctance, he touched on two moral shortcomings, sadly prevalent: no adequate conception of the sanctity of the spoken word; and jealousy among fellow-workers—feelings which prevent effectual combination in the national cause. I would ask the attention of Indian friends to the full text of what Mr. Hume said on this occasion with regard to these shortcomings. The faults referred to are not of a heinous order; but, with fatherly anxiety, he spoke strongly regarding them, because he believed that such defects seriously barred the progress of those whom he regarded as his children.

### SOCIAL REFORM.

But while thus strenuous in his admonition with regard to defects which he specially deprecated, he did not lose sight of the general conditions essential to national progress in India, among a people with customs and traditions originating from an ancient civilization, though modified by foreign aggressions, and by the influences of modern thought. His attitude was judicial; and he recognized that any specific social reform was only one portion of the great work which sought the regeneration of India on all lines, spiritual, social, political, and economic. With the foresight of the experienced organizer he pointed out that success could only be achieved if all reformers—however diverse their specific objects—worked in combination, with a due sense of proportion, and a reasonable regard for existing conditions. These views are set forth in a letter which was published in the *Indian Spectator* of the 1st of February 1885. It is entitled "A letter to Mr. Behramji M. Malabari on the subject of his notes upon Infant Marriages and Enforced Widowhood, and generally on the present prospects and methods of National Progress"; and is so important, both as illustrating Mr. Hume's attitude of mind towards social problems, and as indicating the practical course of action which he favoured, that I have reproduced it *in extenso* as Appendix II. To supplement the views therein stated, another letter is added, Appendix III, regarding the resolution passed by Lord Dufferin's Government with reference to Mr. Malabari's demands for social legislation. In this letter he pointed out that Lord Dufferin's objections to legislate were not unreasonable; and that so long as the Viceroy had virtually only European colleagues as advisers, the Government, however sympathetic it might be, was not in a position to pass measures on such intricate social matters. It is neither good for the commonalty, nor safe for the Government, that foreigners should deal with questions affecting so closely the innermost domestic life of the people. "But," as pointed out by Mr. Hume, "as soon as we have a strong independent representative element in all our Councils, the situation will be altogether changed." Now, happily, under Lord Morley's reforms, a move has been made in the right direction; a representative element has been introduced into the Legislative Councils; and already the independent members have put their hands to the plough. By supporting Mr. Gokhale's Bill for free and compulsory elementary education, they have sought to prepare the soil in which good seed may be sown. Looking to the views expressed by Lord Dufferin, it is an irony of fate that the opposition to the Bill comes from the headquarters of the official camp. The excuse put forward is that the measure is unpopular. But of this there is no evidence whatever. No popular protest has been forthcoming, as was so emphatically the case when the people demonstrated against the Partition of Bengal. On the contrary, the Indian Press is unanimous in support of the Bill, and public meetings in its favour have been held in all parts of the country. The official obstruction discloses what seems to have been an unsound mental condition among the Governors and Lieutenant-Governors who were consulted. On the one hand, in their reports, they claim to know the mind of the people better than the people themselves; on the other hand, they show little effective sympathy with the "heart-felt wish" of King George, who desired to see "spread over the land a net-work of schools and colleges." The official majority in the Viceroy's Council has been employed to destroy Mr. Gokhale's Bill, which followed the most approved methods of dispelling illiteracy among the masses, and would have laid a solid foundation for social reform.

These letters (Appendices II and III) are also valuable as illustrating Mr. Hume's power of adaptation. For it will be remembered that in his great scheme of national regeneration, the original idea was to give the first place to social reform. But his logical mind soon grasped the fact that in India social legislation was not practicable, except with the help of representative institutions. He therefore abandoned his original intention, and, to use his own phrase, devoted his life to political rĕform. And his foresight has been justified by events. For although, in the Viceroy's Council, Mr. Gokhale's Bill was killed by a mechanical majority, the force of argument was altogether with its supporters, and the spirit evinced in the debate is a bright augury for future progress.

### Electoral Campaigns in Dulwich.

On his final retirement from India, Mr. Hume made for himself a quiet little home, a few miles from London, at "The Chalet" in Kingswood Road, Upper Norwood, whence he carried on a constant correspondence with friends in India, while supervising the work of the British Committee at Palace Chambers. To his house he added a spacious studio or working room, beautifully adorned with Indian trophies, where his leisure moments were spent in the scientific pursuits that were so dear to him. But besides these occupations, a ready sympathy with his surroundings led him into vigorous co-operation with the social and political work of the Parliamentary Division of Dulwich, in which he resided. This Division has always been regarded as an impregnable stronghold of Tory "villadom," but this tradition only stimulated in him the *perfervidum ingenium Scotorum,* and again and again he led the Liberal forces to the attack. Naturally the leadership of the people's party had come into his hands, for in him was the root of the matter—"Trust in the People"—"the faith," as he said, "in which I was reared, a faith which has never faltered, a faith, despite the shortcomings of individuals, in the goodness and wisdom of the people as a whole, and in the certain and ultimate triumph of the people's cause, as of all other true and righteous things." His faithful co-worker, Mr. Seth Coward, the Secretary of the Liberal Association, has kindly supplied the following account of his inspiring activities :

"Dulwich, with Peckham and North Camberwell, constitutes the Parliamentary Borough of Camberwell, one of the boroughs carved in 1885 out of the old Parliamentary Borough of Lambeth. Five years later, some time after his retirement from official work in India, Mr. Hume settled in Dulwich and at once threw himself into the work of educating and organizing the constituency with all the force and vigour of his powerful intellect. Mr. Hume was a Radical intensely in earnest, who believed that his time, his wealth, and all his powers were given him in trust for his fellow-creatures.

"The year 1891 saw Mr. Hume hard at work in the constituency. He was elected president of the Dulwich Reform Club, vice-president of the Dulwich and Penge Liberal and Radical Association, and a member of the Executive Council of the Association. During the election of 1892 he acted as the Chairman of the Election Committee for Mr. Arthur Clayden. Sir John Blundell Maple, who had succeeded Mr. Morgan Howard in 1887, was again successful. As might be expected, this defeat only stimulated Mr. Hume's efforts. At the beginning of 1894 he was elected President of the Liberal Association, and held the office till he passed away.

"For many years Mr. Hume was a constant attendant at the meetings of the Association and presided over the meetings of the Executive Council. With the wonderful charm of his magnetic personality he inspired the oft-defeated Liberals with some of his own intense faith in Liberal principles and their ultimate triumph. A profound believer in the reign of law instead of force, of arbitration instead of war, intensely in earnest in giving to the poorest the advantages of education, equality of opportunity for all was with him a passion. All the movements of the day for the improvement of the lot of the poor of our great city found in him a strong supporter. The progressive policy in London and the country was to him the inseparable outcome of the radical changes which he so ardently desired to see in the laws of the country. The abolition of the Veto of the House of Lords was the absolutely indispensable preliminary to Radical measures which he urged again and again. Except the Lords were ended or mended he held that the reform of the land laws, equitable taxation, equality before the legal tribunals, electoral equality, one man one vote, Home Rule for Ireland or India, the abolition of the caste spirit in the Army and Navy and in the Civil Service would never be accomplished: that the Lords' Veto condemned the Liberal Party to a perpetual ploughing of the sands; that till the Liberal Party could pass its measures when in office the work of earnest men to improve the condition of the masses would be in vain. In this spirit Mr. Hume continued the work of organizing the forces of progress in Dulwich.

"On the death of Sir John Blundell Maple in 1903, Mr. C. F. G. Masterman, now the Under-Secretary for the Home Office, contested the division. This was a short, sharp fight, into which Mr. Hume threw himself with characteristic energy. The Conservatives, however, retained the seat. Shortly after, Mr. David Williamson was selected as the Liberal candidate. Mr. Hume took part with him in the most active and vigorous campaign which the constituency had seen. Meetings, indoors and out of doors, were held at frequent intervals. A systematic canvass of the division was made, in which Mr. Hume took a large share of the work of speaking and interviewing. At the General Election in January 1906, Mr. Williamson was defeated by 357 votes only, a result largely due to Mr. Hume's long-continued and inspiring work.

"Perhaps one of Mr. Hume's greatest gifts was his great power of securing the enthusiastic and harmonious co-operation of all classes of Liberal workers. Discord was unknown in the presence of his unselfish devotion to the cause of progress.

"Mr. Williamson again carried the Liberal banner in May of the same year, and Mr. Hume, as the chairman of the Election Committee, was at work early and late. The result, however, was another defeat of the Liberals. From this time Mr. Hume's health did not allow him to take the continuous share of the work he had done. On several occasions he asked the Association to find him a successor for the office of President, but the universal feeling was that, while Mr. Hume lived, no other President was possible. For the last four or five years he has only occasionally taken the chair at the meetings of the Executive Council.

"On reaching his eightieth birthday, the Vice-Presidents of the Association invited all the members to a special garden-party in honour of Mr. Hume. At perhaps the largest gathering of Liberal workers ever held in the constituency the following resolution was passed unanimously and with much enthusiasm :—

"'The members of the Dulwich Liberal and Radical Association (supported by the members of the Dulwich Women's Liberal Association and the Dulwich League of Young Liberals) most heartily congratulate our revered President, A. O. Hume, Esq., C.B., on his attaining his eightieth birthday. They thank him sincerely for his able and generous leadership for the past twenty years, for his uniform kindness and courtesy, and for his example as a high-minded politician. They trust that he may be spared to witness further triumphs of the great Liberal and Radical principles for which he has so fearlessly and consistently fought both in England and India.'

"The selection of Mr. H. E. A. Cotton, the son of his old friend Sir Henry Cotton, as candidate for Dulwich at the General Election in January 1910, was a source of much gratification to him, and, in spite of ill-health, he did much in that vigorous campaign. In December of that year he presided at the meeting of the Association when Mr. Evan Spicer was chosen to fight the Liberal battle, and in various ways assisted Mr. Spicer in his self-sacrificing attempt to win Dulwich for Liberalism.

"Even during his illness, when unable to bear the strain of many personal interviews, he wrote encouraging and inspiring letters showing his still active interest in the work in which he had been so long engaged. This loving interest was shown particularly in the selection and introduction to the constituency of the present Liberal candidate, Mr. C. R. Cooke Taylor. Mr. Hume's illness was brightened by the knowledge that many of the measures whose principles he had advocated for so many years had become law."

## THE SOUTH LONDON BOTANIC INSTITUTE.

This memoir, as a narrative, must conclude with his work in a branch of natural science which, until his later years, he had not systematically explored—botany, the study of "every herb that sips the dew." Mr. W. H. Griffin, Curator of the South London Botanic Institute, which he founded and endowed, has been so good as to prepare an expert statement of his labours in this connection, labours which would have alone filled up the life of an ordinary man. In order to verify the existing catalogues of local plants, he used to spend his summer holidays in some important district, such as Devon, Cornwall, Upper Teesdale in Yorkshire, and the Peak in Derbyshire; and on one occasion I visited him at Looe, where he was engaged in personally investigating the Cornish flora, detecting the appearance or disappearance of local rarities, "escapes," and "undesirable aliens." Owing to its almost insular position, with its mild and moist climate, Cornwall offers peculiar features of interest to the botanist, and the flotsam and jetsam of the numberless vessels coming up the Channel from distant lands, constantly bring strange seeds to germinate in the creeks and harbours of the rocky coast. To stroll in converse with him over cliff and moor was in itself a liberal education. Also at his home I was sometimes privileged to see him at work, in his "peaceful hermitage"; to watch his beautiful manipulation of the dried specimens; and to note the zeal he inspired in his co-workers. Mr. Griffin writes as follows regarding the Botanic Institute:

"I have thought it well in the first place to state the circumstances under which Mr. Hume first engaged me as his botanical assistant, because an illustration of the benevolence of his character is thus afforded.

"In and previously to the year 1900 I had contributed to a Kentish newspaper a weekly article on natural history subjects, many of which were descriptive of the flora of West Kent and East Surrey. Early in 1900 I received, through the editor of the paper, a letter from Mr. Hume, to whom I was then unknown, stating that he desired to add to his herbarium specimens of the orchideous and other plants mentioned in my articles, and requesting me to name a time and place where he could see me. This resulted in Mr. Hume calling upon me at my residence in a south-east London suburb, and an arrangement was made that I should collect and press for Mr. Hume specimens of all the more valuable species I could find, and from time to time send to him in Cornwall, where he was proposing to spend the season in collecting plants, lists of what I might collect, he engaging to defray my travelling and other incidental expenses.

He explained that upon principle he never purchased plants gathered in Britain, because such a practice sometimes led to the extirpation of rare species, and I quite accorded with his views in that respect.

"I was then engaged in business in the City of London, but from April to October in that year I devoted every Saturday afternoon, and frequently the whole of Sunday, and each of the bank holidays, exclusively to collecting plants for Mr. Hume. At this time I was also the honorary secretary of a natural history society which, in co-operation with a few friends, I had assisted in forming in 1897. At the end of October 1900, my health broke down, and I was the recipient of much kindness and help from Mr. Hume until, in the spring of 1901, my strength was somewhat restored, when he engaged me as his botanical assistant.

"I had been accustomed to botanize in the country about the village of Down, in Kent, where the late Dr. Darwin resided during the last forty years of his life; and in April 1901 I took Mr. Hume to certain spots at Down and in the Vale of Cudham, which had been Dr. Darwin's haunts and where he obtained many of the plants mentioned in his famous work on 'The Fertilization of Orchids.' In the same month I also accompanied him to Saffron Walden, in Essex, to collect specimens of *Primula elatior*, a plant which in England grows only upon the chalky boulder-clay. Our only information was that it grew somewhere to the north-west of the railway station, and we proceeded along a road in that direction. I had for many years devoted attention to geology, and perceiving on a roadside bank of clay some worn fragments of rock which I knew were foreign to Essex, I pointed them out to Mr. Hume, with the remark: 'We are on the boulder-clay. Those stones were brought here by ice.'

"Mr. Hume at once appreciated the inference, and I then learned that in his youth he had studied geology, and had known Dr. Mantell, who first discovered remains of the Iguanodon and other Saurians in Wealden Beds, in Sussex. At this period I also accompanied Mr. Hume to Hawkhurst, in Kent, to obtain specimens of *Cardamine bulbifera*. These outings proved to me that Mr. Hume possessed the ready perception of a naturalist experienced in field work. Many who have limited their study of the natural sciences to the library and laboratory are quite at a loss in the field. I have pointed out a rare plant growing amidst other herbage to more than one such student, and they have failed to detect it until their eyes were within two or three feet of it.

"When I first became assistant to Mr. Hume he informed me that if he lived long enough to accumulate a sufficiently large collection of plants his object was to establish an institute to assist amateur botanists whose business occupation did not permit them to resort to the British Museum of Natural History and to Kew Gardens to consult the botanical libraries and herbarium specimens there deposited. In my own experience as an amateur I had found that, while I could generally identify indigenous British plants with the aid of Bentham and Hooker's 'Flora' and Babington's 'Manual,' the alien species frequently met with as garden-escapes and accidental introductions with farm seeds, fodder, etc., occasioned me great difficulty and loss of time; and upon my representing this to Mr. Hume, he decided that his herbarium should comprise all species recorded as having been found quasi-wild in Britain.

"To obtain specimens of the latter he obtained catalogues from German botanists and purchased many sheets of specimens. Some of these were carelessly pressed; others had been grown in Continental gardens, and as I had

had considerable experience as an amateur horticulturist Mr. Hume ultimately allotted to my use a considerable portion of the garden attached to his residence. Seeds were obtained from the Royal Botanic Gardens, Kew, and from similar establishments in France and Austria, and the growing of alien plants for preservation as botanical specimens became a portion of my work, in which Mr. Hume took a deep interest. He delighted in showing these alien plants to his friends and in telling them where the species had been found in a quasi-wild state in Britain.

"At the end of April 1901, Mr. Hume went to Cornwall to continue the collecting of Cornish plants which he had commenced the previous year, and he remained there until October. He made a large collection that year, frequently being assisted by Mr. F. H. Davey, F.L.S., the author of a most excellent flora of Cornwall published in 1909. From May to September 1902 Mr. Hume collected on Dartmoor and the neighbouring parts of Devon, and through October in North Cornwall. In May 1903 he went to Upper Teesdale, Yorkshire, and remained there collecting until October, working during a small portion of the time with Mr. H. W. Pugsley, F.L.S., and Mr. H. S. Thompson, F.L.S. In 1903 Mr. B. T. Lowne, my co-secretary of the Catford and District Natural History Society, exhibited at the Congress of the South-Eastern Union of Scientific Societies some mounted plants, and upon the same sheet with each flowering specimen was a seedling of the species.

"During the congress Miss Ethel Sargent, F.L.S., a well-known experimental botanist, made public reference to the few mounted seedlings, and said that if any botanist would take the trouble to grow and preserve at different stages a comprehensive collection of seedlings it would be invaluable for reference. I submitted the suggestion to

Mr. Hume, and after some demur at the labour which it would entail, and because neither he nor I would live to complete it, he consented to my starting it in the spring of 1904. The herbarium now contains mounted seedlings, taken at progressive stages, of 1200 species, representing 385 genera and 64 natural orders. As a collection, so far as we know, it is unique in Europe, and it is being added to every year as seeds can be obtained. The addition of horticulture to my herbarium and clerical work rendered it necessary to obtain additional assistance in mounting plants and cataloguing, and when the herbarium and library were removed from Mr. Hume's residence we were employing four young women in pressing, mounting, and clerical work, and a youth as assistant in horticultural work.

"During the summer of 1904 Mr. Hume made frequent short excursions into Kent, Surrey, Sussex, etc., to collect species in which the herbarium was deficient. In 1905 he collected plants in Somersetshire, Gloucestershire, and South Wales from April until May, and in North Wales, in company with Mr. C. P. Hurst, one of the most active of English field-botanists, from June to October. In 1906 he was at Folkestone in August and September, and collected largely in that part of Kent. In 1907 he made Eastbourne his headquarters during August and September, and did much field-work in company with the late Mr. T. Hilton, of Brighton. In 1908 he only left home during the month of September, when he went again to Folkestone. In 1909 and 1910 he was at Eastbourne during August and September, and made many excursions for collecting Sussex plants, frequently in company with Mr. Hilton.

*A Gift to South London.*

"In 1910 Mr. Hume purchased the freehold premises, No. 323 Norwood Road, S.E., and adapted them for the reception of his herbarium and library, and the garden fitted for growing the remaining alien plants required for the herbarium. The whole establishment was removed there in November of that year, and the freehold premises, with the herbarium, library, and all appliances and furniture, and a capital endowment to provide an income sufficient to maintain the establishment, were vested in trustees and incorporated under the title of 'The South London Botanical Institute,' with the object, as stated in the registered articles of association, of 'promoting, encouraging, and facilitating, amongst the residents of South London, the study of the science of botany.'

"Mr. Hume had strong objections to advertising, and more especially to advertise his own bounty; and for that reason would have no public opening of the institute, but he somewhat reluctantly consented to the issue of a prospectus to natural history and kindred societies informing them that the herbarium and library were available for the use of their members gratis. When I first became Mr. Hume's assistant he impressed upon me the fact that, as a rule, the preparation of plants for herbarium specimens was done in an inartistic and sometimes slovenly manner, whereas there was no reason why every sheet should not be made to look like a picture. He instructed me in his own painstaking method of laying out and pressing specimens, which I have adopted and passed on to the members of our staff who now perform the work. The following incident illustrates the result. With Mr. Hume's full approbation I have for several years exhibited a selection of our specimens at the annual congress of the South-Eastern Union of Scientific Societies. Upon one of these occasions the specimens were seen by one of the trustees of the British Museum (Natural History). That gentleman told me that the specimens were quite a new departure in herbarium work, and that there was nothing to equal them in the various collections at the Museum.

"In the several occupations in which I have been engaged I have had considerable experience in mechanical work of various kinds, and I soon found that Mr. Hume also was very ready at devising mechanical appliances. Between us we designed a system of iron racks and cabinets for the herbarium by means of which specimens of any species are immediately accessible; and I believe our system is to be adopted in one department of the British Museum of Natural History.

"When I joined Mr. Hume in 1901 his British herbarium consisted of between 2000 and 3000 sheets. There are now more than 40,000 sheets of these plants, every one of which passed through Mr. Hume's hands for critical examination before it was mounted.

"The late Mr. Frederick Townsend, F.L.S., an eminent botanist, who died in 1905, left instructions that after his death his herbarium and botanical library should be given to Mr. Hume for the purposes of the institute, which was then in contemplation; and in February 1906 Mr. Hume took me with him to Honington Hall, near Shipston-on-Stour, Mr. Townsend's former residence, to arrange for its transfer to Norwood. After this, until the end of 1911, every moment which Mr. Hume could spare from other duties was occupied by him in going through the general collection of European plants formed by Mr. Townsend and giving them out for mounting. Then, in 1910, the late Mr. W. H. Beeby, F.L.S., another eminent botanist, who had formed what is probably the only collection of North Isles (Shetland and the Orkneys) plants in Europe, also left instructions at his death for that and his other collections to be made over to Mr. Hume.

"Incessant industry was Mr. Hume's own practice, and he very naturally expected every one about him to follow him in this respect. He was intensely impatient with anything approaching idleness or lack of interest in their work on the part of those whom he employed, but, at the same time, most considerate and generous in the case of sickness. Those who knew him best could not but entertain for him reverent esteem and affection, and we who constituted his botanical staff feel that we have lost not only a considerate employer, but a fatherly friend."

# EPILOGUE

It would be wrong to close this account of so remarkable a career in the Indian public service without seeking to draw from it lessons for the future wise guidance of Indian affairs. And this seems the more necessary because a Royal Commission has been appointed to consider the requirements of the Indian public service, and to "recommend such changes as may seem expedient." The scope of the reference is a wide one, opening up the whole question of the position and duties of the Indian Civil Service; and the practical questions to be dealt with are, What are the defects of the present system? and What are the changes needed to make it conformable to the best interests of the Indian people?

When we look into the merits of the case, we find that the essential defects of the system belong to its historical origin as a foreign domination, and that these defects have been intensified by the policy of over-centralization, which is the natural development of any purely official organization. As regards origin, we know that England's first connection with India was not based on any altruistic sentiment; it arose in the earlier centuries out of primitive impulses, the spirit of adventure and the pursuit of gain. Coming originally as traders, the servants of the East India Company became administrators by the force of circumstances, as the only means of evolving order out of the anarchy which prevailed in India at the close of the eighteenth century. Autocratic personal government was thus both unavoidable and beneficial in the early years of British rule; and Lord Cornwallis, by a judicious reorganization, laid the foundations of the "Covenanted" Indian Civil Service which, on the whole, has shown itself the most efficient and most honest official body of which there is record. But, as the poet warns us, the old order changeth, and one good custom may corrupt the world. The conditions which necessitated, and justified, an official autocracy administered by a privileged class of foreigners, have long passed away; highly trained Indians are available for every branch of the public service; while public opinion claims for the people a revival of the ancient forms of local self-government.

As regards the later history of the official system, the one development of paramount importance has been the gradual rise of the great centralized departments till they have become the chief power in the State; and it will be necessary to note their action on the different branches of the Indian administration, for to their usurpations is due the over-centralization which has proved destructive alike to local administration and to the control which should be exercised by the Secretary of State and the House of Commons.

The main object of Liberal statesmen, as shown by the policy of Lord Ripon and Lord Morley, has been, and must be, to bring these overgrown departments into proper subordination, and limit them to their proper functions. And fortunately, in dealing with this problem we possess, in the events of Mr. Hume's career, materials for forming a judgment with regard to the effects of over-centralization upon the working of the public service in its various grades. In order to show these effects, I proposed, at the beginning of this memoir, a practical test by which the merits, and demerits, of the present system of administration may be judged. In Allan Hume we have the ideal public servant—capable, industrious, and devoted to the public interests; a man regarding whom the Government record testifies that he "sacrificed all personal considerations to the conscientious discharge of his duties." A good system would naturally welcome such a man in every grade of the service. If metal of this temper cannot be utilized in the official machinery, the fault must be with the machinery. Let us apply this test, first to the district administration, in which Mr. Hume was a striking success; and secondly, to the Simla Secretariat from which he was summarily ejected.

While the village community is the social unit, the District or Collectorate has always been the unit of the official administration; and District Officers are the backbone of British rule, provided they possess adequate authority, and are in touch with the people. In the case of Mr. Hume these conditions were in great measure fulfilled. In those early days the Collector occupied a strong position as the local representative of the "Sirkar" in all departments; and Mr. Hume, relying on the co-operation of the people, and the friendly counsels of his local friends, was master of the situation, whether in the stress of the Mutiny, or in the peaceful activities of a later period. As a local Akbar, in free communication with the people, he understood their requirements, and could promote economic developments according to the special needs of the District. Unfortunately the centralizing policy has barred further progress; instead of strengthening the position of the Collector on a popular basis, it has gone far to destroy the powers and usefulness of the district administration, by transferring the executive authority from the district officers to the subordinates of the centralized departments at headquarters.

Thirty years ago, when Lord Ripon was taking up the subject of local self-government, these great centralized departments, and their fatal encroachments, were thus described by one who knew: "Their name is legion: police, public works, forest, excise, salt, survey, irrigation, registration, sanitation, vaccination, and so forth. Each of these departments is represented in the rural districts by a swarm of ill-paid and hungry native subordinates, who prowl about the villages and gradually fatten themselves by plunder and oppression. Among all these departments and among all these petty oppressors the life of the poorer ryot may be likened to that of a toad under a harrow, so jarred is he and upset in all his dearest interests and prejudices. And it is the increasing irritation and unrest produced throughout the country by years of such a system which has hitherto constituted the real danger to our rule in India. Now at last efforts are being made to stop this daily torment, to give back to the Indian village communities the management of their own internal affairs. And we need not wonder that the ryot is glad and grateful. It must be borne in mind that, whatever system we follow, the actual details of administration must be done by natives. And the special purpose of the decentralization and local self-government measures now being brought forward, is to substitute the best kind of native agency for the worst; to revive the ancient activity of rural municipal life, and to entrust the village management to the decent quiet villagers themselves instead of leaving it to a swarm of greedy underlings attracted to the Government service, not by the scanty pay, but by the power they enjoy, and the unlimited opportunities for exaction." Octopus-like these centralized departments extend their tentacles into every district and every village, paralysing the district administrators, and crushing the village organization. Decentralization is the remedy; and this remedy Lord Ripon sought to apply by the only right method, that is, not by the multiplication of local autocrats, but by building up local self-government on the solid foundation of the village community.

I have likened the centralized departments, in their destructive action on the district and village organizations, to the grasp of the octopus. But if on the one hand the deadly tentacles have reached down to the ryot in his village, they have, with equally baneful effect, taken hold of the supreme Government at Simla and the Council of the Secretary of State at Whitehall, perverting to their own use the control of the House of Commons. They have thus been able to direct policy, and manipulate the Indian Legislature, which for many years has been simply an instrument for consolidating official authority. What is the object of the elaborate codes which, with ever increasing stringency, govern the operations of the Land Revenue, the Forests, the Excise, and other great departments? Every one knows that all these codes originate with the department directly interested, and that they are all directed to increasing "efficiency," which means the perfecting of the official machine, and completing its domination over the outside public. Indian public opinion has little or nothing to do with the course of legislation: it is only consulted after the supreme Executive has made up its mind under the direction of the department interested. Hence the government of India has been called a tyranny of office boxes, only mitigated by an occasional loss of the key. It is in these office boxes that projects of law are incubated, and that ingenious devices are matured to close all loopholes of escape, and effectually to curb the liberty of the subject.

The Viceroy, being a statesman appointed from home, is the one powerful figure that is in a position to offer resistance, if so minded, to the coercion of the permanent departments. But he will not be so minded if he is tainted with the imperialistic spirit, or if he has not the necessary courage and ability. In any case the task of resistance is a hard one, as shown by what befell Lord Canning, Lord Mayo, and Lord Ripon ; for the Viceroy stands almost alone among his Councillors, who for the most part have themselves been the heads of departments; while in England he must count on secret hostility, instead of support, from the India Office, which is recruited from the ruling official clique at Simla. The two notable episodes of Mr. Hume's career at the Simla Secretariat, which have been already related, were connected with two Viceroys of very different characteristics, and these episodes illustrate forcibly the sinister power of bureaucratic influences. In the one case Lord Mayo's strong personal recommendation in favour of an Agricultural Bureau, with Mr. Hume at its head, was rejected owing to the combined opposition of officials at Simla and Whitehall ; while in the other case official hostility, with the sympathetic help of Lord Lytton, was able, without cause shown or even alleged, to oust Mr. Hume from a high office, for which admittedly he had special qualifications. The usual history of Viceroys and Governor-Generals has been this : when they have sought to hold the balance evenly, they have suffered obloquy and defeat ; when their sympathies have been racial and imperialistic, the occasion has been utilized to fortify and extend the domination of the European bureaucracy.

The causes from which these evils spring are deep-seated. The fault is not in the men, whose average character and abilities are of a high order, but in the system, which places them in a position antagonistic to popular aspirations ; which gives them autocratic power without effective control ; which stimulates selfish ambition, and penalizes independence of judgment. The treatment of Mr. Hume at headquarters resulted naturally from the hostility of the class of men who, under the existing system, are the most successful in reaching the top of the official ladder ; and for this the system is to blame. But in order to understand the unholy spirit generated in the inner official clique at Simla, it is necessary to bear in mind the conditions which govern recruitment and promotion in the Indian Civil Service. The old Company's system of nomination and training at Haileybury College, which kept the Civil Service in the hands of families traditionally connected with India, had its defects, but it also tended to maintain among the members of the service a certain atmosphere of friendly sympathy with the people. This atmosphere of sympathy was dissipated by the adoption of competitive examinations, which brought into the service a new class of men, self-confident, ambitious, and usually unconnected with India. These young men, coming to India fresh from their academic studies, without experience of English public life, and placed almost at once in positions of authority over men of another race, form exactly the material needed to produce an extreme bureaucrat. Nor does their subsequent experience in a close service tend to correct the failings appurtenant to this character. For the conditions of promotion to high office are peculiar, owing to the violent oscillations of policy to which the Government of India is subject. At one time we have adventure abroad and retrogression at home, under Lord Lytton, followed, under Lord Ripon, by a return to Lord Lawrence's policy of masterly inactivity on the frontier, with masterly activity in domestic progress. It is evident that a man of strong convictions and independent character, cannot serve these two masters with equal zeal and equal claim for advancement. Mr. A, who is an honest admirer of Lord Lytton's Imperialism, must lie low under Lord Ripon, while Mr. B, who is an enthusiast for local self-government, will be out in the cold when the "forward" policy is in the ascendant. But Mr. X, who has no strong convictions either way, comes under no such disqualifications. He is equally ready to serve both masters; either to gag the Press, or to free it; either to befriend the leaders of the people, or to put them in gaol for sedition. To his mind, these are questions of policy, for which he is not responsible; his business is to carry out the orders of Government; if he does not do so, some one else will; he will be superseded by a junior, and his chances of distinction will be lost. Such sentiments are abhorrent to men of the type of Mr. Hume. But to Mr. X they seem a mere matter of official business. "Let who will be king," he gets his promotion, going up two steps of the official ladder for one step gained either by Mr. A or by Mr. B; he becomes the chief of a centralized department; and passes early into the group at headquarters who are eligible to be members of the Viceroy's Council and Lieutenant-Governors. Thus, by a process of natural selection, is formed the dominant Simla clique, which controls the Government, disregarding public opinion, and trampling on the rank and file of the service. Naturally enough, the members of this Junta and their adherents take the pick of official prizes; decorate themselves as a matter of course; and ultimately co-opt each other into the Council of the Secretary of State at Whitehall, where they sit in secret as a Court of Appeal from India, and pass favourable judgments on their own past achievements, and those of their friends.

### The Public Service Commission.

*Decentralization in India.*

Such is the condition of affairs with which Indian reformers have to deal. A great opportunity is afforded by the appointment of the Royal Commission on the public service; and it is hoped that Congress leaders will make the most of the occasion, tracing the defects of the present system, and placing before the Commission a well-considered scheme, showing the changes needed to make the Indian administration conformable to the best interests of the Indian people. Decentralization on a popular basis is the cardinal principle for the reform of the public service, and Lord Ripon's policy of local self-government should be carried out to its legitimate conclusions. Over-centralization must therefore be attacked in all its ramifications, as it affects the village and district organizations on the one hand, and as it affects the supreme Executive on the other. Fortunately the evils of the present system have already been recognized emphatically by the highest authorities; and in 1909 Lord Morley appointed a Royal Commission to examine into the "great mischief of over-centralization," and to enquire how "this great mischief might be alleviated." The reference was admirable, and excellent results would have followed, if the Commission had possessed the element of judicial impartiality. But in the composition of the Commission there was no such element. A grievous mistake was made in the selection of the Commissioners, all of whom belonged to the class directly interested in maintaining the existing system.

Of the six members of the Commission only one was an Indian, Mr. Romesh Dutt, while all, including the chairman, were of the official class. Independent Indian opinion was therefore wholly unrepresented. And this initial defect was aggravated by the fact that the three Anglo-Indian civilians, who constituted half the Commission, belonged to the class of headquarters officials who are little in touch with the people, whose views generally differ from those of the rank and file of the service, and who are mainly responsible for the existing over-centralization.

As might have been expected, the Commission was a failure. Nothing was done to promote local self-government on a popular basis; on the contrary, some of the recommendations in the report were of a retrogressive character; and the great mischief recognized by Lord Morley remained without alleviation. But though its conclusions were impotent, the Commission recorded some valuable evidence of Indian witnesses, notably that given by Mr. Gokhale on behalf of the Bombay Presidency Association. Mr. Gokhale showed that local self-government must be built up on the natural foundation of the village community; and, as in old times, the "Pancháyat," or village council, should have the management of all matters pertaining exclusively to the village. As regards the district administration, the chief proposal was to strengthen the position of the District Officer by giving him a small District Council, partly elective and partly nominated, which he would be bound to consult on all important occasions. Large additional powers might be delegated to him, provided these powers were exercised in association with his Council, so that ordinary questions of administration would be disposed of promptly on the spot, without unnecessary reference to higher authorities. If such additional resources had been at the disposal of Mr. Hume as a District Officer, the lot of Etawah under his administration would have been indeed a happy one.

These are the lines upon which reform should proceed with regard to local self-government. But while dealing with specific grievances, regard must be had to the larger responsibilities belonging to the new era which has been opened out for the Indian people by Lord Morley's reforms, and by the Delhi declarations of King George. The existing system, under which a few hundred foreign officials govern autocratically a population of 250 millions, is obsolete. A very material change must be made in the official fabric; the edifice requires to be remodelled from the foundations to the roof, from the village organization to the ultimate control by the House of Commons. And a change is also needed in the spirit of the administration: Trust in the people must be substituted for trust in bureaucracy. Public servants must be the servants of the public; not its masters.

*Control in England.*

But there will be no security for popular rights unless provision is made for an impartial and effective control in England over the Indian Executive. Mr. Fox's Bill, a hundred and thirty years ago, proposed to effect this by placing the control in the hands of a strong and independent commission appointed by Parliament from among the most trusted public men in England, men unconnected with the Indian administration, and prepared to enforce publicly and with judicial impartiality the broad principles of justice and good government. This was the scheme so eloquently supported by Edmund Burke, who "desired to regulate the administration of India upon the principles of a Court of Judicature, and to exclude, as far as human prudence can exclude, all possibility of a corrupt partiality, in appointing to office, or covering from enquiry and punishment, any person who has abused, or shall abuse his authority." As a move in this direction some practical reforms might now be adopted, as recommended in the Minority Report of Lord Welby's Commission. As regards the responsible advisers of the Secretary of State, it was proposed (para. 34) that "a sufficient number of representative Indians of position and experience should be nominated to the Council of the Secretary of State on the recommendation of the elected members of the Viceroy's and Local Legislative Councils." Perhaps, as a beginning, representative Indians, selected in this way, might constitute not less than one-third of the Council; another third being officials; and the remaining third being selected from "the most trusted public men in England," unconnected with the Indian administration.

As regards control by Parliament, the recommendation of the Minority Report ran as follows: "In the time of the East India Company a Parliamentary enquiry was held every twenty years, before the renewal of the Charter. From these enquiries date the most important reforms for the benefit of India. Also the prospect of such an enquiry tended to check abuses. This old practice should be revived by statute." Further, "in order to maintain the controlling authority over Indian expenditure, the salary of the Secretary of State for India should be placed upon the British estimates." And in order to give reality to the "Indian Budget debate," the House of Commons should each year appoint a Select Committee to enquire into and report upon the financial conditions of India, as shown in the Budget, and in the discussions thereon in the Legislative Council of the Viceroy. Lord Morley has told us that we should realize "the enormous weight, complexity, delicacy, and hazards" of our obligations towards India. The measures above suggested would do something towards giving Parliament the knowledge and opportunity needed to fulfil its duties as trustee for the Indian people.

### CONCLUSION.

It was, I think, Thomas Carlyle who said that old age was "dark and unlovely." But this was not so with Mr. Hume. Even under physical suffering, there were for him elements of brightness and beauty. For his mind to him a kingdom was: up to the last he was actively engaged in the scientific pursuits which were always his special joy; and his eyes were privileged to see, though in the dim distance, the salvation of India. To use his own expression, he had a "great and enduring Hope" for the future of India; and he said that if he could only live to see that Hope realized, he would "die content and happy." His labours are now bearing rich fruit, and it has been a consolation to his sorrowing friends that, before he passed away, he had the assurance that a happier day was dawning for the people that he loved so well.

On the 31st of July 1912, in his eighty-fourth year, Allan Octavian Hume passed peacefully away. His funeral at Brookwood Cemetery was simple; and the words on his monument were few. But far away, among the millions of India, there was deep sorrow. In telegrams, in letters, and in Resolutions at public meetings, the feelings of the people throughout the land were expressed in touching language. Some of these are given in Appendix IV. No one could have had mourners more multitudinous, or more sincere. For his name and his good deeds were known in the remotest villages of

India; and everywhere the people came together to lament the loss of a friend, who had laboured for them, who had suffered for them, and who had shown them the way of national salvation. The *Leader* of Allahabad, in its issue of 31st August last, published a most interesting note of reminiscences (reproduced Appendix V) by Mr. Zorawar Singh Nigam, a Municipal Commissioner of Etawah, in which he revives memories showing "what Mr. Hume's name means in the city and district." Though half a century has elapsed the people have not forgotten his good works, and on the news of his death the shops in the Etawah Bazar were closed as a mark of respect. At the Hume Memorial Meeting the Collector, Mr. H. R. Neville, presided, and spoke feelingly of the progress and prosperity of the district under his administration.

When we look back upon Mr. Hume's career, and his noble scheme for the harmonious evolution of East and West, we are reminded of the culture hero of Greece—Prometheus, the spirit of progress, "he who thinks forwards"; withstood in all ages, and among all races, by Epimetheus, "he who thinks backwards," the prototype of blind authority, which learns nothing, and forgets nothing. Prometheus brought the sacred fire from heaven, to endow men of clay with spiritual life; and taught them the arts and sciences, bringing upon himself the vengeance of the ruling powers: he suffered for the people, but triumphed in the end, when Hercules slew the vultures that preyed upon his vitals, and unloosed his bonds. In every nation the same struggle goes on between progress and autocracy, between enlightenment and obscurantism; and it is well for India that her destiny is linked with England; and not with Russia, where the spirit of the people is crushed by a dull and deadly bureaucratic despotism. In England, the ancient home of freedom, those who trust in Russian methods can only prevail for a season; and for India's future we may well share in Allan Hume's assured Hope that though sorrow may endure for a night, joy will come in the morning.

# APPENDIXES

## APPENDIX I

ETAWAH, *24th July*, 1860.

To G. R. HAYWOOD Esq.
*Secretary to the Cotton Supply Association,*
*Manchester.*

DEAR SIR,—

Your letter and circular, dated December 1859 only reached me on the 17*th of the current month*—with whom the delay rests I cannot say—I at least am not in fault.

Fully concurring with you in the importance of increasing the quantity and improving the quality of the cotton grown in these provinces, I have for years given the subject as much attention as I could spare from my other multifarious duties, and am therefore in a position to answer most of the Queries put by you.

At the same time, lest, seeing how unsatisfactory many of my replies necessarily are, you should be disposed to wonder or cavil at my not having taken more energetic measures, to further the objects that I with you admit to be most desirable, allow me to remind you, that to an officer, to whom the entire government of six or seven hundred thousand people is confided, an improved or enhanced growth of cotton, can at most be but a very secondary object, to which time and attention can only be devoted, after weightier matters, such as the securing protection to life and property, the establishment and maintenance of schools, hospitals, and public libraries, the realization of Revenue, the construction of Public Works, etc., etc., have been duly provided for.

And now to reply to your queries seriatim—

1. The cotton plant *is* grown in this, the Etawah District.

2. There is only one kind of cotton now grown in this district, I enclose samples, in the boll and cleaned. The former may be taken as a fair specimen of the best average cotton here grown—the latter will enable you to judge how far the Churkha here in use injures the fibre. The quality of the produce depends very much on the soil and season and fully half of the Etawah cotton is (taking the average of several years) inferior to the enclosed sample—on the other hand about 10 per cent. is superior.

3. No cotton of the American variety is grown here, nor would there appear to have ever been any vigorous efforts on a large scale to introduce its cultivation. Some few of the Zemindars seem to have tried a few acres of it some twenty-five years ago, but it took they allege so long to flower that the bolls never rightly came to maturity. I myself have sown it for three successive years without any success. I have so little time for gardening that I fear the cotton (though I saw it planted myself on the most approved form of ridge, and subsequently moulded and hilled) did not get properly looked after. Perhaps however the seed was in fault—the people here usually call the American variety "Nurma Kupas" or soft cotton.

4. Last year we had 57,675 acres of land under (cotton) cultivation and the produce amounted to 107,929 maunds or 8,634,320 lb., showing an average yield of only 150 lb. per acre; but the rains were very defective, and I think I shall not be wrong in assuming 250 lb. as the average yield per acre, in a fair season, of our average good land when reasonably carefully cultivated.

5. See No. 3.

6. Our soil varies in different parts of the district from very light sandy earth ("Bhoor" as it is here called) to a rich but still not clayey loam (known as "Do mut"). The climate is that of the rest of the districts of the central Duab—but perhaps a little warmer than some of its neighbours in January and February, cold at night and in mornings

and evenings the temperature is often below freezing-point—in the middle of the day it ranges from 80° to 94° in the sun; towards the end of February the heat increases and in March and the first fifteen days of April the temperature gradually rises, so that by the end of March the thermometer may be said never to fall below 65° and to rise to 110° at midday. During the latter part of April, May, and June till the first showers of the rain fall the heat is very great and the hot winds blow more or less continually. The thermometer very rarely, even just before sunrise falling below 80° and at 2 p.m. rising to 120° *in the shade* (we had it above that in our tents in 1858) and to 140° and even more incredible heights if exposed to the sun—however, towards the middle or end of May we sometimes have a little heavy rain which for a time cools the air. During June or early in July the periodical rains commence and continue with more or less violence till the end of August or the middle of September. The temperature during these months (dependent chiefly on the amount of rain that falls and the manner in which the falls are distributed) varies so much in different years and at different parts of the same season that it is difficult to give it any numerical representative, but perhaps if I assume 86° as the lowest and 112° as the highest average temperature in the shade during the rains, I shall not be far wrong. After the rain ceases there is usually a month of very hot and steamy weather, but during the course of October, the nights begin to grow cool, and the latter half of November and December are almost as cool as January. There is usually a fall of rain about the end of December which lasts a few days. The total fall of rain during the whole year is I estimate on the average 28 inches, of which 22 fall during the Rainy Season.

7. The cotton seed is usually sown during June after the first or second good fall of rain, but it is also at times (especially if the rains are late) sown in dry ground and there left to await the expected showers.

In years in which the rains are favourable, viz., in which the total fall is pretty equably distributed throughout the three months from 15 June to 15 September, no irrigation is required or resorted to. But when there is a failure of rain during the early part of the season the people irrigate wherever they can; but if the rain still holds off irrigation is generally abandoned as too expensive and of little use. The out-turn is best when the rains cease a little before the plant flowers, which is on the average 75 days from the date of sowing in wet earth, or of the first good shower if sown in dry. The produce is scarce and of an inferior quality when rain falls on the flower, and still more so when it falls on the pod. We reckon a lightish loam best suited to cotton, and find that manuring it adds much more to the produce than it would in the case of wheat or barley—hence what little manure the people take the trouble to collect and cart is usually devoted to cotton lands. Irrigation is available in about one fourth of the district from the Ganges Canal (or will soon be when all the minor irrigation channels are complete) and in about another fourth from wells, tanks, rivers, etc. The people as a rule believe that irrigation neither improves the quality nor increases the quantity of the produce.

8. Clean cotton is on the average one-third of the total picking, that would give for last year only an average of 50 lb. per acre and in good years 80 lb. In this district three times the land now under cultivation could be easily devoted to the growth of cotton.

9. Nothing would be easier than to extend the cultivation, if set about in a proper way. What we chiefly require are money advances, increased intelligence and a ready and *good* sale on the spot (see further No. 12).

10. The only obstacles are want of capital and intelligence and the extreme uncertainty of the demand (see further No. 12).

11. Of the produce of this district we estimate that not *more* than one-third is consumed by the natives of the district itself, but that of the remainder not more than 2,000,000 lb. is exported to England, the rest being absorbed in Bengal.

12. There are no European merchants in this or any of

the surrounding districts who purchase or as far as I can judge would purchase cotton. Nor are there any native merchants who purchase cotton on a large scale. Radhe Lall, Bhugwan Dass and Umrao Singh are the chief native cotton purchasers of Etawah, but they together scarcely purchase £10,000 worth per annum. Some twenty-five years ago Messrs. Wright and I think Ritchie at Agra, and Mr. Bruce at Calpee did a good deal of business in this line, here and in the neighbouring districts—and Mr. Bruce was a cotton planter as well as purchaser. All seemed to have failed. This was long before I came to this part of the country, and I cannot therefore offer any opinion of my own as to the causes of their want of success, but if any reliance may be placed in native accounts, their failure was due to causes independent of the trade in which they were engaged. Mr. H. H. Bell of Oomergarh, in the Muttra district, also I *believe* some fourteen years ago, tried (at the request of the late J. Thomason Esq., Lt.-Governor) the experiment of growing American cotton and purchasing the native variety, but he too would seem to have found the business unprofitable. You ask what agency should be employed to purchase cotton and send it home to England. I would suggest that the Association send out to Etawah some member of one of the large Manchester firms whose name would be a sufficient guarantee for the character of his transactions. That this gentleman should establish here a regular agency for the purchase and factory for the cleaning and pressing of cotton. This should be bought raw and cleaned under his own supervision—a good steam Pratt gin, for instance, would increase the value of the cotton 15 per cent. and save 5 per cent. in labour, while if fuel became ultimately any difficulty, as it possibly might, cattle, horse or mule power might be used as in the States. The cotton so bought and cleaned should be pressed, packed, and sent off from here to England (in boats to Calcutta by the Jumna). The cotton agent might at the same time gradually introduce better kinds of cotton, keeping up a small model farm both with the view of ascertaining which varieties are best for this part of the country, and which is the most advantageous mode of growing them, and also for the purpose of keeping up a supply of acclimatized seed for distribution and giving the growers practical lessons of how to improve their husbandry. Moreover as the produce increased the agent could gradually introduce good hand gins, and get a great deal of the cotton well cleaned by the people themselves. Besides the produce of Etawah itself, a factory at Etawah would command the whole produce of the very extensive cotton field of which it is the centre and which includes a great portion of Dholpoor, Agra, Muttra, Mynpooree, Furrackabad, Cawnpoor, Jalown, and the North of Gwalior. I don't hesitate to say that with two or three years of liberal, just, and ready-money transactions 25,000,000 lb. of *clean* cotton could be easily sent home annually from here, and if a system of advances to intending cultivators was adopted, I should not despair of multiplying the amount many times. The business would require capital, temper, time, intelligence, and liberality, and what is not common in India, regular *business* habits—but it would, I believe, be very profitable, and a few such agencies in India judiciously located would I believe enable our merchants in Manchester to command an almost indefinite supply of cotton of *any* quality that the physical conditions of soil and climate permit the growth of. What the highest quality here obtainable really is time and repeated experiments on a considerable scale, by men who know exactly what to try and how to try it, alone can show, but that the present standard can be very considerably raised even without the introduction of new varieties, I have myself twice practically proved. Even supposing that no cotton better than the sample sent were to be usually grown here, the scheme I propose would I conclude be remunerative. At present, the *grower* sells it to a petty dealer, after having "mangled" it with an infamous "churkha" that very seriously injures the fibre, the petty dealer sells it to a native merchant, who packs it (without any press, and so badly that it has to be repacked down country), and exports it sometimes direct to Calcutta, but more often only Mirzapoor; and then it passes through one or two more hands before it is finally shipped for England. Surely the direct agency properly managed, by which the cotton is cleaned without injury to the fibre, packed at once and exported without there being any middleman to absorb the profits, would be amply remunerative when the present ill-managed system affords profits sufficient to support five or six different parties.

Cotton of the quality of the raw sample herewith sent might I calculate on the average, if bought in large quantities, cleaned by good gins, properly packed and sent down the Jumna in boats, be put on board ship at Calcutta at Rs. 10 8 ans. per maund, or at £1 1s. per 80 lb. avoirdupois, or 3·15 per lb. (exclusive of cost of agency and risk of insurance). The question is what will the freight home cost, and what would the average value of cotton of the quality of the raw sample herewith sent be in Manchester if it had been properly cleaned by a good gin?

I must however note that the price of cotton here is liable to most extraordinary fluctuations; at the present moment if I had to buy cotton, clean it, etc., it would cost (even supposing I had all the means and appliances above suggested) at least 4½ per lb. before it got on ship board at Calcutta. This I take to be owing in great measure to the extreme uncertainty of the demand. Were there a regular agency for its purchase here, I do not think the price would vary as much as it now does or average higher than that above quoted.

13. The actual price of the cotton cleaned at Etawah is usually under the present retail system about Rs. 7 12 ans., or 15s. 6d. (it is much more at the present moment) per maund of 80 lb., but if bought and cleaned by horse or steam gins, on a *large scale*, would, besides being much better, stand in some 8 ans. or 1s. less. It costs now 8 ans. or 1s. to pack one maund of it very badly—with a good screw press it could be packed so as not to require reopening till it reached England for 4 ans. or 6d., and it is carried from here to Calcutta in boats via the

Jumna to Allahabad, and thence by the Ganges and Hooglee for Rs. 3 or 6s. per maund, whereas, if properly packed, it would certainly cost 8 ans. per maund less in transit. We have therefore—

| | At present. | | | | | As suggested. | | | | |
|---|---|---|---|---|---|---|---|---|---|---|
| | Indian. | | English. | | | Indian. | | English. | | |
| | Rs. | as. | £ | s. | d. | Rs. | as. | £ | s. | d. |
| Cost of cotton of quality of sample cleaned at Etawah, per maund of 80 lb.... ... ... ... ... | 7 | 14 | 0 | 15 | 9 | 7 | 6 | 0 | 14 | 9 |
| Packing ditto ... ... ... ... | 0 | 8 | 0 | 1 | 0 | 0 | 4 | 0 | 0 | 6 |
| Carriage to Calcutta ... ... ... | 3 | 0 | 0 | 6 | 0 | 2 | 8 | 0 | 5 | 0 |
| Cost at Calcutta of maund or 80 lb. | 11 | 6 | 1 | 2 | 9 | 10 | 2 | 1 | 0 | 3 |

I would add that though, allowing for contingencies, I have in answer No. 12 stated the price per maund of 80 lb. at Rs. 10 8 ans. or £1 1s., I should myself be sanguine of reducing this average if the business were conducted on a sufficiently large and liberal scale.

14. Etawah is admirably situated as a locality for a cotton agency—it is built, as the map will show you, on the banks of the Jumna, thus ensuring cheap and uninterrupted water carriage to Calcutta. It has moreover a good road from Gwalior on the one hand (crossing the Jumna and Chambal, over both of which I have established bridges of boats) and to Furrickabad on the Ganges on the other; the main railroad from Allahabad and Calcutta to Agra, Delhi and the Punjaub passes through it, and though two years will probably elapse before that portion of the line lying between Raj Mehal and Allahabad is entirely complete the section from Allahabad to Agra will it is believed be open to the public in less than a twelvemonth. Besides this I have during the last three years constructed some 400 miles of good cart roads leading from all parts of the district to the town of Etawah itself, so that really the only way in which

the means of conveyance could, as far as I can see, be improved would be by the construction of a better class of barges for the transport of the cotton by river. These should I think be iron, and built in compartments. The sinking and burning of the boats now in use are a source of great loss.

15. The growers have only the common seed. If really good seed were furnished them numbers would be *glad* to buy it on a small scale at first and if it succeeded on a large scale afterwards. The fact is that as far as my experience goes, Hindoos like Englishmen, are perfectly ready to take any good advice or adopt any good plan, if you can only demonstrate to them practically that *it pays.* That is the touchstone. If the higher quality for any reason does not *pay* them so well as that they now grow, they will after a few trials abandon it—if it *pays better* you may depend on their sticking to it. One thing that is necessary for the successful growing of the foreign varieties is a short practical manual, *drawn up with reference to the requirements of this country and these provinces.* Louisiana and Alabama are *not at all like* the North-West provinces of India, and prize essays on the cultivation of Orleans staple cotton in the Valley of the Mississippi, are believe me but of little value in Etawah no matter how "experienced" the "planters" from whom they emanate. A good practical manual such as we require could be best compiled after a few years of experience at an Experimental Farm of the kind alluded to in my twelfth answer.

16. The native "Churkha" is the only instrument here used at present and they have no press for baling it. The cotton is packed for the market in the most primitive fashion imaginable. Bags of a cylindrical form, about 4 feet long by 3 feet in diameter, open at one end, are suspended (so that the bottom is about a foot off the ground) by four or more ropes run through the edges of the mouth or open end, to a like number of poles firmly planted in the ground round about the bags. The cotton is then thrown in little by little, and a man standing inside the bag keeps steadily treading it

down till the bale is full—such bags usually contain 3 maunds 5 seers, or 250 lb. of cotton each. There is a smaller kind also in use here which weighs when full only about 150 lb.

17. The cost of cleaning cotton by the "Churkha" is 3 or $3\frac{1}{10}$th of a penny—a man who receives 2 ans. or 3d. per diem cleans 5 seers or 10 lb. in a day. The seed usually sells for about 10 per cent. more than the cost of cleaning.

18. Samples of the cotton here grown both in the raw state and cleaned are put up.

19. I have no seed that I can depend on. This year I have got a little from the Calcutta Agri-horticultural Society, which if it succeeds will enable me to distribute a little seed next year, but if the Association choose to furnish me with a considerable quantity of first-rate seed, I will undertake to get it tried in many places of the district and if it succeeds to have the seed so raised distributed on a large scale; but it must be distinctly understood that such seed must reach me free of cost and that I cannot myself go to any expense in cultivating it as I have already too many schools, libraries, and other district institutions *entirely* dependent on me, to undertake any new scheme at present.

20. Samples of the cotton fabrics of this district (with the prices in English and Indian money and other particulars on labels attached to them) are herewith forwarded.

21. In this district there is but little waste land and this latter is (with the exception of a few hundred acres, scattered about in tiny patches) altogether barren and unculturable.

22. I have unfortunately no time at present to discuss the gigantic question of "how the general trade and commerce of the district may be most effectually extended," and in regard to the one particular branch of commerce in which the Association must be chiefly interested I have, I think, already nearly sufficiently taxed your patience. Let me however be again reminding you of the extreme difference both of climate and soil between these provinces and not only the Valley of the Mississippi but also the Southern and Central portions of India itself. New Orleans cotton whether culti-

vated according to American or Indian practice has hitherto succeeded but indifferently in these provinces, but who knows what success some combination of the two or some entirely new system of culture might lead to? On the other hand supposing it to be proved impossible to bring the American variety to perfection here, it is by no means improbable that the African or still better the Egyptian might succeed. What is required is experience—an experimental farm carried on on a liberal scale under a really able and educated man for half a dozen years, would probably settle the matter as regards the cotton field of which Etawah is the natural centre. If the Association really wish for this experience, really desire to improve the quality and increase the quantity of cotton grown here and elsewhere—they must put their own shoulders to the wheel—give up memorializing Government, and do what they want done themselves—at their own expense. In the long run they will find it the cheapest and best plan.

I need hardly say that any agency of the nature suggested by me in my twelfth answer, would meet with my most willing support, and that I should be at all times ready to afford any advice or assistance that my long residence in this district and intimate acquaintance with its people rendered me qualified to give.

I am, dear sir,
Yours faithfully,
A. O. Hume.

PS.—The Macarthy gins would be readily purchased here, if the people could be convinced that they answer. If one as a specimen were sent with full instructions as to use, and I could show them practically that it was a *paying* investment, there would be no difficulty I fancy in disposing of five hundred like it in a single year.

*Note.*—As ill-health compels me to go on leave for a few months any reply you may wish to send should be addressed to me *by name to the care of* the Magistrate and Collector, Etawah.

## APPENDIX II

### A LETTER TO MR. BEHRAMJI M. MALABARI,

ON THE SUBJECT OF HIS NOTES UPON INFANT MARRIAGES AND ENFORCED WIDOWHOOD AND GENERALLY ON THE PRESENT PROSPECTS AND METHODS OF NATIONAL PROGRESS.

(*Reprinted from the "Indian Spectator" of February* 1, 1885)

My dear Malabari—

I have read with the most entire sympathy your cogent and eloquent Notes on the evils attendant on infant marriages and enforced widowhood. Privately, for years past, I have strenuously urged on Native friends the necessity of reform in these and other kindred social matters; so that you must not attribute my long delay in answering your letter, enclosing these papers, to any want of interest in the painful subjects to which they relate. Most entirely do I agree with you, that much misery results from these customs; that in the present day (whatever may have been the case in times long past), the evil generated by them far outweighs any good with which they can justly be credited—that yearly this disproportion will increase, and that their abolition is even now an object in every way worthy to be aimed at.

There is so little genuine unselfish enthusiasm in the world nowadays, that agreeing thus far with you, I have been unwilling to appear in any way to throw cold water on your zeal, by tendering only a qualified concurrence in your views. But since you continue to insist on a public confession of the faith that is in me, I must in justice to the great national cause, which we both alike have at heart, say distinctly, what—rightly or wrongly—I really think about the matter.

In the first place I must say I think you *somewhat* exaggerate the evil results of these traditional institutions. I quite admit that there is full warrant for everything you advance—the terrible evils you refer to are real; but they are not, to my idea, by any means so universal as the ordinary reader of your Notes would, I think, be led to infer. Moreover, though I admit that the evil does, on the whole, outweigh the good, it is not fair to our people to allow it to be supposed, that they are so hopelessly blind as to cling to institutions which are utterly and unmitigatedly bad. In the existing state of the Native social problem, no really impartial competent judge will, I believe, deny that in many cases these institutions even yet work fairly well. There are millions of cases in which early marriages are believed to be daily proving happy ones, and in which consummation having been deferred by the parents (and this, my friends say, is the usual case) till a reasonable age (I mean for Asiatic girls) the progeny are, so far as we can judge, perfectly healthy, physically and mentally.

A Native friend writes to me, "The wife, transplanted to her husband's home at a tender age, forgets the ties that bound her to the parental hearth, and by the time she comes of age is perfectly naturalized in her adopted family; and though she is allowed no wifely intercourse with her husband until she attains a fitting age, still the husband and wife have constant opportunities of assimilating each other's natures and growing, as it were, into one, so that when the real marriage takes place the love they feel for each other is not merely passion, but is mingled with far higher and purer feelings. Misfortunes cannot alienate our wives, they have no frowns for us, even though we commit the most heinous crimes or ill-treat or sin against themselves. Those ignorant of our inner life call this a vile subjugation and say that we have made our wives our slaves, but those who live amongst us know that it is the result of that deep-seated affection that springs from early association and religious (if you will, superstitious) teachings.

"Where will you find a wife so true and contented as a Hindu's? Where more purity of thought or more religious fervour than in the Hindu women of respectable families? Our men, alas! may be materialists, atheists, immoral, base, but our women are goodness in human shape—and why? because they have been shown an object on which to concentrate the entire love and veneration of their natures at a time when their pure hearts were unsullied by any other impressions or ideas, and taught to look up to their husbands, whose faces they could only look on after many solemn ceremonies, as their guardians, protectors, and gods."

Everything in this world has its darker and brighter sides and the blackest cloud has some silver lining; and though my friend in his happy husbandhood (for his has been, I know, a happy infant marriage) generalizes too enthusiastically from his own experience, still he has some foundation for his contention; and infant marriage (though fraught with grievous misery in too many cases, though a custom marked for extinction and daily becoming more and of an anachronism and more and more of an evil, taking its results as a whole), has not yet become that unmitigated curse, unrelieved by redeeming features, which, forgive me if I say so, your vigorous onslaught would, it seems to me, lead the European reader to believe.

Do you remember "Uncle Tom's Cabin"? There was not one incident recorded in that novel, in connection with the grievous iniquities of slavery, for which actual warrant did not exist, and yet the general result was to produce a grossly exaggerated picture of the working of the system. Many look upon that highly coloured narrative as the first seed of the subsequent emancipation of the slaves; personally, I credit it mainly with the perfectly needless slaughter of about half a million of persons. It took hold on the mind of the nation. It grievously angered the Southerners, many of them the kindest and best of masters, beloved beyond measure by their so-called slaves, who, seeing themselves and their institutions wantonly maligned, became all the more resolutely determined to oppose any reform (prior to this numbers of the Southerners were themselves considering how emancipation could be gradually brought about). It grievously inflamed the righteous indignation of the New Englanders, and a certain better-minded section of the other northern States—and it led to John Brown and his marching soul and all the "battle, murder, and sudden death" that followed. You will be told that the North and South fought over the tariff, and so a large section of the northern States unquestionably did, but these would never have ventured to provoke or accept (for this is a moot point) a civil war, but for the enthusiasm of the honest anti-slavery party. But for "Uncle Tom's Cabin," I fully believe that slavery would have been abolished before now, and without any civil war.

But works of fiction attacking social evils always, it may be said, exaggerate the case, and Charles Reade and Charles Dickens will be pointed to as having equally picked out individual instances of wrong and so presented them as to make them appear the necessary and inevitable results of systems which, as a matter of fact, by no means invariably led to such serious consequences.

But even if such exaggeration be permissible in works of fiction, and if this high colouring does really do good *in the long run* (which is at least an arguable point) by attracting and concentrating attention, it certainly does not do this, in my opinion, in the case of grave prosaic State papers, like yours, and rightly or wrongly, my experience and inquiries lead me to believe that in your righteous indignation against wrong and desire to get rid of what is evil, you have depicted that evil in blacker colours than the facts of the case, *taken as a whole*, really warrant.

As regards the question of enforced widowhood I have *in limine* a somewhat similar objection to take. It is productive of great evils, much unhappiness, much demoralization. It is a custom against which common-sense, and all the best instincts of our nature write, as in the case of slavery, the verdict "*delenda est.*" But with all that, it does not, taking the country as a whole, produce so much evil as might be theoretically inferred. It is bad enough doubtless, but it is not that gigantic cancer at the heart's core of society, that tremendous and cruel evil, the eradication of which is essential as the first step to national regeneration, that the casual reader unacquainted with the intricacies of social life in the East, might well conceive it to be from your eloquent and earnest denunciations.

But besides this I have another difficulty. I must divide widows into titular or virgin widows, and real widows. As to the former I have satisfied myself by a careful study of all the authentic and authoritative texts produced on both sides, that there is nothing in the Shastras to prevent *their* re-marriage; and there being positively no good that can be even alleged as resulting from enforcing their continued widowhood, while very grave evils unquestionably flow therefrom, I have no hesitation in earnestly pressing and entreating every good Hindu, who loves his family, his fellows or his country, to combine to make re-marriages in such cases *customary* and thus, as it were, *legislate for themselves* on this matter.

For the re-marriage of fully married or real widows, I cannot say as much. I entertain no doubt that according to the Shastras, the re-marriage of such involved a loss of caste. I regret that this should be so, but I believe it to be the case, and being so, I could press no Hindu brother, who conscientiously accepts these ancient writings, not merely as the teachings of eminently pious *men* (and therefore necessarily imperfect, suited only to the time in which they were written and open to correction in the light of a more advanced civilization), but as the immutable commands of the Almighty —I could, I say, ask no such Hindu to do violence to his conscience by transgressing what he believes to be the laws of God, even were the evils resulting from this enforced widowhood tenfold what they are.

# Appendix II

Such I would only pray by sympathy and watchful care, by tenderness and love, to mitigate so far as may be the lonely lot of the poor women that they are compelled by religious convictions thus to isolate, and by educating *all* their women, and elevating their mental and moral status, to minimize the inevitable evils, resulting from this enforced, and in the cases of young women, unnatural widowhood. As for those fellows, whose whole lives, redolent of fraud, falsehood, greed or gluttony, show plainly how little *they* regard the Shastras, and who yet seize upon texts, out of sacred writings (every other command of which they disregard when it suits their own purposes) to justify the retention, as ill-used household drudges or unacknowledged concubines, of the poor women entrusted to their care, they are hypocrites whom I hope all brother Hindus, orthodox and unorthodox, will combine to reward as they merit.

No! let the real believer, who lives honestly and truly by his Shastras, still keep his widowed daughter or daughter-in-law, unmarried according to his creed—in such a house, no harm will come to her. It may seem hard upon the poor girl—but in a truly pious household trials are but the seeds of future glories. But let the hypocrite who, whenever he seeks the gratification of his own vices or passions, disregards the sacred commands he pretends to accept, though making a great show of reverencing them *when it suits his purpose*, remember, that call it by what name men will, there *is* a retribution for all wrong and that he shall surely himself suffer for all the suffering he causes, and for all the sin and sorrow this may evolve.

In the second place, besides holding that obnoxious as are the customs against which you take arms, you have somewhat exaggerated the magnitude and universality of the evils to which they give rise, I cannot but fear that your method of thus attacking particular branches of a larger question, as if they could be successfully isolated and dealt with as distinct entities, is calculated to mislead the public, to confuse their conceptions of proportion, to entail loss of power and intensify, what seems to me at this present moment to be, the most serious obstacle to real National progress.

I do not ignore the fact that in our practical work we may and often must, adopt the moral of the fagot fable and proceed to break the sticks one by one, but we must all, from the outset, realize the entire fagot and set before us as our ultimate aim and end, not the fracture of the one stick but the destruction of the entire bundle.

But to me it seems that you put forward these two unquestionably desirable reforms as if they were the most momentous questions of the day, and as if on them hinged the national regeneration, whereas they are mere fractional parts which can never be successfully manipulated by themselves, and which even if they could be so treated, would not, independently of progress in other directions, produce any very marked results upon the country as a whole.

The tendency of your Notes must be, I fear, to give all your readers a somewhat exaggerated and disproportioned idea of the importance of these matters, themselves only branches of the larger question of raising the status of our women generally, itself again only one of many essential factors in National progress.

Moreover, pressing these isolated points so strongly, as if they were obligatory and stood by themselves, and not as mere optional sections of a general enterprise, has certainly temporarily alienated some who would cordially have co-operated in many other sections. Now we cannot afford to alienate a single possible coadjutor, and it is only by starting on a platform co-extensive with the aspirations of the country that we can hope to secure the co-operation of even the majority of that powerful (though numerically small) body of earnest workers who have learnt to look in one direction or another, outside the sordid veil of "self" that still darkens the perceptions of their brethren.

The earnest and unselfish labourers for Progress in this country constitute but an infinitesimal fraction of the population, a fraction that becomes absolutely inappreciable if further subdivided. If, then, any real results are to be achieved, it can only be by linking together all those who love the light and would fain push the darkness farther back, in a common effort against a common evil.

Doubtless, division of labour is the seed of Progress, and throughout the universe specialization goes hand in hand with development. We may expect different minds to devote themselves more especially to different sections of the work, but they must be taken up as integral parts of the whole, subordinate portions of the common enterprise in which all are interested.

As it is, in consequence of the all-pervading spirit of division of labour, the minds of our reformers are, as a rule, too exclusively turned to individual abuses and too little in sympathy with the aspirations of fellow-workers struggling against other forms of wrong ; and our first aim should be to infuse a spirit of catholicity into the entire body of those willing to labour, in *any* direction, for the common weal.

It is essential, I think, that we should all try to realize that closely interwoven in humanity as are the physical, intellectual and psychical factors, progress in any direction, to be real or permanent, postulates a corresponding progress in other directions—that though we may and must most specially devote our energies to overcoming the particular adversary that circumstances have most immediately opposed to us, we each form but one unit in a force contending against a common foe, whose defeat will depend as much on the success of each of our fellow-soldiers as on our own. In the hour of battle it signifies nothing whether a man is in the light or grenadier company, the whole regiment must advance—the individual can do little ; it matters not whether one is in the cavalry, artillery, infantry, pioneers or what not, the success of each is the success of all, the defeat of any an additional obstacle to the triumph of the rest.

At present the greatest impediment to all progress here appears to me to consist in a general failure to realize the essential unity of the cause of reform. You find earnest men whose eyes appear to be closed to everything but the material wants of the people, and to whom the poverty of our population appears to be the one sole evil against which it is necessary to concentrate all efforts. You find equally devoted enthusiasts who see in the ignorance of the masses the source of all their sufferings and in their intellectual elevation a panacea for all woes. You find men of the purest and highest aspirations, careless to a great extent of both the material and mental wants of the nation, making their sole aim either its moral development or religious culture. There are some of your social reformers who hold that India is to be saved by the abolition or modification of some evil or obsolete custom or habit, and nailing this flag to their own masts are willing to see the rest of the fleet sink if only their ships forge somewhat ahead. And last but not least, you have the strong practical men, who Gallio-like care for none of these things but place all their hopes on the realization of their aspirations for the political enfranchisement of their countrymen.

What we want, it seems to me, at the present time most of all, is that all these good labourers should understand that they are comrades in one cause, that their aims, though diverse, are not only not antagonistic, but are inextricably interlinked parts of one whole—that if you could multiply tenfold every peasant's means you would serve the country's interests but little did you not simultaneously elevate the mental and moral faculties, so as to secure a wise, prudent, and good use of the money, root out old customs involving its rapid dissipation, and confer such a political status as would enable the owners to preserve and protect their newly found wealth—that no great development of brain power is possible on empty stomachs and where men's whole energies have to be devoted to simply satisfying the cravings of these, and that even if possible it would become a positive evil if unaccompanied by moral or spiritual evolution, and by means for gratifying the necessarily resulting political aspirations—that moral culture is best fostered, mankind being what it is, by removing from men's paths those terrible temptations to evil engendered by poverty, hunger, and natural envy of those more fortunate, and that the hope of attaining to the exercise of political functions is often one of the strongest incitements to a higher morality—that the extinction of a few evil customs will avail little without a thorough recast of the social framework, a thing only possible as the result of a general advance along all the other lines, physical, intellectual, psychical and political—and that lastly, nations in the long run always get precisely as good a Government as they deserve, and that no nominal political enfranchisement will in practice prove more than a change of evils unless such an advance has simultaneously or antecedently been made along all these other lines as shall render the country qualified to assimilate its improved political status.

Now, whether rightly or wrongly, it seems to me that a sporadic crusade such as the one you have now undertaken —not to capture the Holy Land, but merely to destroy one little stronghold of the infidels therein—is an utter waste of power, in so much that even if crowned with momentary success, it could have no permanent result while the hills that command it and its water-supply are still in the hands of the enemy. It would be like our capture of the Redan before the Mamelon was in our allies' hands.

And I think further that such isolated crusades have a distinct tendency to intensify that sectarianism in Reform which, as I have already said, seems to me the chief obstacle to progress. And when you threaten, as you often do, to abandon all other work and devote for the rest of your life your great abilities and energies, your fearless honesty and fiery enthusiasm, to these two comparatively minor matters, you seem to me, I confess, like a man who should concentrate all his attention and efforts upon a single plank in the bottom of his ship, leaving all the rest to wind and wave, to rock and rot, as Chance may will it.

No doubt specialization goes hand in hand with development; but national reform here is still in the amœbic stage, and no such specialization as this would imply is as yet practicable. We all remember the statesman who was said to have given to a Party the talents designed to serve mankind. Would you, following this erring example, give to two minor questions those powers designed to serve the national cause as a whole? Believe me, it would be not only to inflict on your country an irreparable loss—for there is no other single man whose services she could less easily spare—but it would be a sin against your own soul, like his who hid his talent in the napkin.

One single example will bring home to any thinking mind the extent to which the country suffers, by this premature specialization, and by the absence of co-operation and sympathy, and the lack of unity of purpose, amongst even true would-be reformers, working in different, and even in the same directions. In this age of materialism, when existing faiths, Eastern and Western, seem alike losing all vital hold upon the hearts of their votaries, when the glamour of this material world seems to blind mankind to the existence of other states, of which this present life is but an infinitesimal fragment—when "eat and drink and be merry, for to-morrow we die," seems almost the only *living* creed—there is no one more important question than that of the moral and spiritual culture of the nation. Morality is the sole rock upon which national prosperity can be securely based—all other foundations are but as shifting sands. The old safeguards of national morality here are crumbling into ruin. To teach men once more the beauty and happiness of pure lives and pure thoughts is perhaps the greatest requisite of all if that national regeneration, for which we all sigh, is ever to be more than a dream. Throughout the length and breadth of the land are scattered, thinly it is true, men, the salt of the earth, Hindus, Christians, Mohammedans and votaries of other innumerable sects—men to whom pure lives and lofty aspirations are as the air to us grosser mortals; who give their time and hearts, and would gladly give their *lives*, to leading other souls along the holy paths that they have trodden to find peace—men who have really one common object, the moral exaltation of their fellows—men who if they could only widen their sympathies and lovingly band themselves in united action with all those fellow-labourers whose real aim, like their own, is the purification of mankind, would in twenty years raise the whole tone of national thought—but who, working on, each in his sectarian groove, not only without aiding, not only without sympathy for, but too often in positive hostility towards those whom they should hail as comrades and brothers, live and die leaving scarcely a foot-print on the soul-sands of the age.

Who can reckon the incalculable loss that the country sustains by this persistent antagonism of forces, which combined, would transform the nation in a single generation? Let us, who labour on a humbler plane, beware how we allow ourselves to drift into analogous dissociation, and pinning our faiths on no one particular reform, no one special panacea, even if we have not ourselves the opportunity of working in all directions, at least aid, sympathize, and co-operate with all who, in any form and in any direction, labour in singleness of heart for the common weal.

The time has not yet come when any of us, few as we are, can rightly take up a single branch of one of many questions and devote to that our entire thoughts and time, careless of all else. Your pet subjects are but side branches of the great question of elevating the status of our women, and cannot, it seems to me, be dissociated, theoretically or practically, from that. The majority of the opposition with which your proposals have been met in certain Native circles has had its origin in the conviction that our women and girls are not yet sufficiently educated to enable any great change in the social customs which regulate their lives to be safely made, at present.

To me personally, the promotion of female education (using the word in its broadest sense) as necessarily antecedent to the thorough eradication of the grievous evils you so forcibly depict, appears a more important and immediately pressing question than those selected by you.

I cannot plead guilty to being a benevolent let-alonist.

I desire to press forward along all the lines, but I am averse to spasmodic onslaughts in isolated directions and I believe that for our entire work, and *à fortiori* for each fragmentary portion thereof, *festina lente* is the true motto.

Having alluded to female education, pardon me if before closing I say a few words on a subject too generally overlooked, viz., the intimate connection that exists between the elevation of the status of our women, and that political enfranchisement for which alone so many of our ablest co-workers think it worth while to labour ; it will illustrate my previous contention as to the essential one-ness of the cause of national reform. I will not argue with my Native friends, who twit me with Divorce Courts and Hill-station scandals, whether our modern so-called education does render European women as a whole less liable to fall. I will not argue with them as to whether, taking households by the million, there is more chastity in the East or the West. Thank God, I have known of thousands of pure households in both—and everywhere so long as this race of man exists, there will be weak women whom *no* education can touch, and wicked men, and whether there be more of these in this or that nation no mortal man is really qualified to judge ; and this moreover is wholly beyond the present question, since *all* will admit that a *properly* educated woman, whose mental and moral faculties have been thoroughly developed, must necessarily be less liable to err than one who remains uneducated. I by no means set up the average education of European girls as all that could be desired—all I ask for is a really good education for all Indian girls, and if the European system is defective let us improve upon it and adopt a more perfect one.

But what I do desire to make plain is that without the proper education of our females, without their elevation to their natural and rightful position, no great and permanent political progress can be hoped for. It is by such education alone that the national intellect can be completed and the East put in a position to compete fairly with the West.

As in the individual there are two brains whose harmonious co-operation is essential to the best mental work, so in the nation are there two intellects, the male and the female, whose equipoised interaction is indispensable to the evolution of a wise national conduct.

The male intellect, however cultivated, still remains imperfect until supplemented by that of the educated woman. Mill's essay on Liberty—his grandest work—owes its perfection, I firmly believe, as asserted by its author, to his long discussions of the subject with a highly educated lady. A nation whose women are uneducated, let its men have all possible culture, still goes into the world's battle with only one arm.

The superiority of Western over Eastern nations (and in many matters this is beyond dispute) is mainly due to the fact that in the former both the female and the male mind are brought to bear upon all great public questions. Ladies, it is true, do not as yet sit in the House of Commons, but there is not a vote taken in that House on any important national question which has not been fully as much influenced by the female as by the male minds of the educated classes.

In a despotically governed country where the Sovereign associates with himself one or more highly intellectual, if perhaps only self-educated women, the evil of the general mental degradation of the females of the country may not so distinctly and directly react on the public policy; but where by the spread of liberal institutions the popular voice becomes, as it is even here becoming day by day, a more and more powerful factor in the direction of public affairs the community which retains its women uneducated and deliberately deprives itself of their intellectual co-operation, can never hope to compete successfully with others in which public policy is the joint product of the cultivated male and female mind.

Political reformers of all shades of opinion should never forget that unless the elevation of the female element in the nation proceeds *pari passu* with their work, all their labour for the political enfranchisement of the country will prove vain; and in so far as the two customs against which you righteously inveigh tend *inter alia* to depress that element, all are bound to sympathize with and support you in your proposed reforms: not overrating their importance, not pressing them too furiously before their time is ripe, but accepting them as two, amongst several, reforms by which our women must be raised to their rightful status, before India, whether still affiliated to England or not, can become either truly prosperous or truly free.

In conclusion I must apologize for the length of this rambling letter and even more so for presuming thus to differ in some degree from one so much better entitled to speak with authority than myself. But you insisted on having my thoughts on the subject, and right or wrong, in all their natural ruggedness, you have them now.

Yours sincerely,

A. O. HUME.

# APPENDIX III

## LORD DUFFERIN'S RESOLUTION ON HINDU REFORMS

*A Letter from Mr. Hume to Mr. M. B. Malabari*

You ask me what I think of the Government Resolution.

I think it a capital one—all you could possibly desire in the present position of the question and more than you could, I think, have expected.

The entire question has been thoroughly thrashed out all over the whole Empire. All that *can* be said upon the question has now been put on record, either in the papers collected by the Government of India from all the several Provinces, which they are now about to publish, or in the many letters which you have elicited from all sorts and conditions of men, which *you* doubtless will also soon publish. There will no longer be, for any one who will study the exhaustive all-sided discussion of the case embodied in these two "collections," any possibility of doubt as to the *facts*. Action will be no longer fettered by the fear that there may lurk unknown difficulties.

The whole thing has been made clear—exaggerations of both sides brought thus face to face will neutralize each other, and the sober facts of the case will stand out clear and simple.

That two of the most complicated and controverted problems of social reform, which for at least a quarter of a century have engaged in a desultory fashion the minds of the public, should thus in three short years have been cleared of all misconceptions and misrepresentation and reduced to their simplest elements, is a great work and one for which the country will, hereafter, I feel sure, be adequately grateful to you.

One thing is now certain—all the best and wisest men in this Empire, without distinction of race, creed or colour, are at one with you as regards the absolute necessity of the great Social Reforms which you advocate.

It is only as to your methods that differences of opinion and, I think, some, misconceptions exist.

You are believed generally to advocate coercive legislation which neither I myself nor, I believe, the majority of Indians are at all prepared to accept. But if I now rightly understand you, all you really look forward to is legislation of an enabling and permissive character. Now even for this the time does not seem to me to be altogether ripe, but I see no reason why, if the agitation be properly kept up and a conviction of the disadvantages of the existing system be steadily forced home to a larger and larger number of minds, something of the kind might not properly be conceded in a few years.

This is how I view the question : If A chooses to marry a widow, or to keep his sons unmarried to eighteen or twenty and his daughters unmarried till they are thirteen, or even fifteen, or seventeen, B, C and D must always be left at liberty to cut A in their individual and private capacities : but this is a different thing from B, C, and D combining as a *Punchayet*, not merely to cut A, but to threaten E and F, who sympathize with A that if they do not straightway cut their friend A they will put them also out of caste.

That A's right of private judgment in such matters and *à fortiori* E's and F's should be protected by "enabling" legislation, appears to me to be by no means too much to hope for. I myself see no reason why when public opinion ripens on the subjects, the legislature should not prohibit *Punchayets* from putting persons out of caste on these grounds, while leaving it free to every individual member of any community to cut or drop any or every other member thereof in his private capacity, as may seem good to him. In my opinion, this is the legislation you should aim at, and the only legislation that could ever be necessary or justifiable. But even this legislation you cannot expect from a Government entirely composed of foreigners. Were I Viceroy at this moment with virtually only European colleagues, I should reply to you just as Lord Dufferin has done, viz., that Government is not in a position to legislate on such subjects. But as soon as we have a strong independent representative element in all our Councils, the situation will be altogether changed, and whenever and wherever a considerable majority of Indian Representatives press for permissive legislation of the character above indicated, then and there, be sure that Government will cease to oppose it. And I confess that until we have such representatives and until these support and press for such a measure, I see little prospect of your obtaining any legislative sanction for the efforts of the Social Reform Party. Now it is to secure this representation that the National or Political Reform Party are straining every nerve, and you and your party, if they are wise, will second their efforts with the heartiest good will. Together we must all rise or together be plunged in the existing Slough of Despond.

It is grievous to find honest patriots working in other lines, because they dissent from some of your methods instead of merely controverting these, descending to attribute to you unworthy motives and to attack *you* personally, than whom (whatever errors you may possibly have fallen into) a more earnest or honest lover of India and her people does not, I believe (and I speak after many years' knowledge of you) exist.

I know that some who attack you thus do not really mean all they say, but merely hope (and a very vain hope it is) to keep you quiet. They say, "Confound the fellow, why can't he keep quiet: what we want first and foremost is political enfranchisement, the fuss he keeps making about his widows, etc., tends to sow dissensions in our camp, and to direct the public mind from the more important work we have in hand,

and in regard to which there is really no difference of opinion amongst us."

But this involves a double mistake. In the first place, though we differ amongst ourselves as to widow re-marriage, there is nothing in such diversity of opinion to prevent our combining, *if we are true patriots working unselfishly for our country's good*, to press as one man for those representative institutions in regard to which we are all agreed. In the second place no great political progress can ever be made unless a somewhat corresponding progress is being made in all other lines. One man must take up political, another social, another mental, another moral, another physical reform. And no one man or body of men can work too hard at, or make too much fuss over, his or their special line of reform, since push ahead as far as he or they may, they will only stimulate the champions of other causes to greater exertions and probably to still further advance in *their* special lines, and thus only amidst this generous rivalry of well doing in a dozen different directions will the nation grow and develop symmetrically in greatness and goodness. Every true son of India, however much he may differ from you as to methods, knows well that the reforms you aim at are noble and necessary ones, and every true son of India ought to feel it to be a sin against his country to say an unkind word against, or attribute the smallest unworthy motive to, one who is struggling so earnestly and unselfishly to advance in one direction that country's cause. I myself have devoted my life to political reform, but I none the less reverence those good and high-minded men who are everywhere (though all too few in numbers) labouring to raise the moral tone of the people, none the less sympathize with those learned and highly-cultured men who are striving to promote their education, or with those hearty honest men who desire by promoting athletic sports and games to raise their physique, and *à fortiori* is my heart none the less with those earnest and unselfish workers who, like yourself, are giving their lives to the cause of social reform. I can understand our differing amongst ourselves as to matters of practice, as to what should *first* be done and *how* to set about it, but I cannot understand such differences degenerating into personal injustice and ill-will ; I cannot understand anything but brotherly love and mutual sympathy between the co-workers in different lines in this one great national cause.

I say God bless all who are working for India.

# APPENDIX IV

THE news of the death of Mr. Hume called forth a remarkable expression of grief from Indians in all parts of the Empire. At a public meeting held in Westminster the Hon. Mr. Gokhale referred to Mr. Hume as "one of those men who appeared from time to time in this world, under the dispensation of a wise Providence, to help forward the onward march of humanity, whose voice sounded like a trumpet-call, waking up whole peoples from the slumber of ages, and whose title to an honoured place in the history of nations no man could possibly challenge. Mr. Hume loved India passionately, as every one who knew him could testify, and he loved justice and freedom also passionately. Thus it was that, after the close of a distinguished official career, he came forward to devote his great gifts to guiding India along the path of justice and freedom and self-respect. He came forward to teach Indians to walk nobly along the path of nationhood."

Mr. D. E. Wacha, Joint General Secretary of the Indian National Congress, wrote in the *Indian Review* that in Mr. Hume "Indians instinctively recognized a commanding personality. To those who had come into close contact and intimacy with him it was manifest that he was an Agamemnon and Nestor rolled into one—such were his force of character, his sagacity and his determined will. His was a unique advocacy inspired by the noblest and most righteous thoughts. He alone knew how to charm, how to strengthen, and how to teach. He is gone, but not without teaching us that though we have no wings to soar, we have feet to scale and climb, more and more by slow degrees the cloudy summits of our times."

Mr. Surendranath Banerjea, in the course of a speech made at Calcutta, said that "Mr. Hume worked in sickness and in health for the political advancement of the people of India with a self-sacrificing zeal and a single-mindedness of purpose which will enshrine his memory in the affections of the people, and will entitle him to the deepest gratitude of the most distant generations of Indians. His name will stand forth in the golden records of Indian history as one of the great builders of Indian national life and one of the truest promoters of Indian national union. . . . In the muster roll of distinguished Englishmen who had laid broad the foundation of the British rule in India and had enthroned themselves in the hearts of the people, Allan Hume would occupy a prominent position. Mr. Hume, in the golden record of Indian history, stood as a successor and lineal descendant of the Metcalfes and Bentincks, and the great band of missionary philanthropists who had sown the seeds of their educational progress, seeds which to-day under the beautiful laws of evolution were bearing such splendid fruits."

Dr. Rash Behari Ghose, speaking at the same meeting, expressed his confidence that "when the voice of blind passion and vulgar strife is hushed, the name of Allan Hume will find a conspicuous place in the roll of those good servants of England who are imperial in the true sense of the term ; for the true imperialist is not the man who shouts the loudest about the imperial destiny of England, but the man who is conscious of the great trust which has been laid on England and which a great and righteous nation alone can discharge. . . . Hume's tomb is the whole of India and his most lasting memorial will be found not in marble or bronze, but in the hearts of those for whom he lived and died."

The Hon. Pandit Madan Mohan Malaviya, speaking at Allahabad, said that "Mr. Hume inspired, elevated and educated those who came under his influence by the nobleness of his nature, his world-wide sympathies, his profound earnestness, his selfless, ceaseless devotion to the cause which he believed to be good and which he espoused, and by his unshakable faith that right and justice would eventually triumph. He was truly a great soul—one of the noblest Englishmen ever born. He was one of those benefactors of mankind who came to initiate movements of great potentiality for the good of their fellow-men. Mr. Hume combined in him the large-hearted love of freedom, of justice and of equality of treatment between man and man. He hated oppression and wrong-doing, and sincerely and earnestly desired the good of all his fellow-men."

The Hon. R. N. Mudholkear, speaking at Amraoti, said, "Misunderstood, misrepresented and reviled by short-sighted or perverse men, he was one of the most potent friends of British rule, a veritable pillar of strength to it. Directing the mind and energies of the thinking portion of the Indian community into the channels of constitutional agitation, he and his co-workers effectually minimized the chance of its flow into unsafe and dangerous courses, while his intense humanity and abiding sympathy for the Indian people deepened their faith in British justice. He was more than a far-sighted and noble Briton or a friend and benefactor of India. He was a saint, one of those beings sent now and then to the earth to rouse men to a due recognition of the higher and brighter side of human nature. In him India has lost a guide, a teacher, a leader, whose every word and every act was instinct with wisdom and deep affection ; England a loyal, high-minded and far-seeing son ; the Empire a statesman-like citizen, and the human race an ardent striver after great ideals."

While the leaders of Indian public opinion referred to Mr. Hume's services in terms of unqualified affection and admiration, the Indian newspapers paid warm tribute to the departed leader. The *Bengalee* of Calcutta wrote that to Mr. Hume belonged "the credit of organizing the scattered elements of public life and focusing them in an institution which was to cement the public spirit of the country, to build and stimulate national life. The first

Congress that met in Bombay in 1885 was a small gathering of leading men, of which Allan Hume was the guiding spirit, but it was the parent of the great National Congress which in the course of the last quarter of a century has revolutionized the political aspect of the country. To-day from the heart of educated India there will go forth a great wail of sorrow at the death of one who helped forward, such as few Englishmen have done in the lifetime of this generation, the political interests of the people of India."

The *Amritza Bazar Patrika* referred to Mr. Hume's character as pure and unblemished, rarely to be found in any other country in the world. He served India without any thought of reward.

The *Indian Mirror* wrote that the "awakening of what is known as the national life of India was due pre-eminently to Allan Hume and his colleagues in the earlier days. It was they who stimulated public spirit and taught the people of India to seek their political salvation by constitutional political work. Advance on the lines of orderly and peaceful self-development was the first article of their political creed. In doubt and difficulty they stood by India like the valiant crew of an ocean liner, cheering and encouraging by hopeful and wise counsel."

A Mohammedan journal (*Comrade*) wrote that Mr. Hume "was one of those few high-souled Indian Civil Service men who devoted their life to selfless service for the people of this country and fearlessly championed the cause of its social and political regeneration at the ready sacrifice of official preferments and honours. But though denied official recognition, Mr. Hume's philanthropic activities for the uplifting of Indians gained for him a warm corner in Indian hearts. So firm was his hold on the confidence of the Indian masses that even in the dark days of the Mutiny their thorough reliance on his justice and kindness was never shaken. Such a life should be a model for our modern Anglo-Indian officers."

The *Leader* of Allahabad wrote: "The sorrow and grief of the hundreds of millions who inhabit this vast and great and ancient land for the venerable departed can be given no adequate expression. An Englishman and a member of the Indian Civil Service, Mr. Hume, with a freedom from prejudice rare as it was glorious, founded the Indian National Congress, an organization of which no Indian can be too proud. If a new life is visible in India to-day, if the Indians have a national self-consciousness which was non-existent before the year of the first Congress, if their national self-respect is higher, if the esteem in which they are held by the civilized world is greater than it was, if with determination and self-confidence they look forward to the day when their country will have responsible government such as is enjoyed by the self-governing dominions of the Empire ; the credit for all this is to no small extent due to the Congress that was founded by Mr. Hume and therefore to Mr. Hume himself. The names of Allan Hume and William Wedderburn will be inseparably associated for ever in the Indian mind as the two worshippable men who laid aside every consideration of self and of race in order to strive nobly and work actively for the regeneration of an ancient land now low in the confederacy of nations but with a rich promise of coming into her own by dint of unselfish exertion persisted in notwithstanding failure, in the simple faith in God that no good cause can fail."

The Lahore *Tribune* said Mr. Hume "corresponded with all public men in India and spent money freely in promoting the cause of the Indian National Congress. He wrote leading articles for newspapers, corresponded with the highest officials, carried on controversies, wrote pamphlets, and was tireless in his industry. He was by no means in robust health, but nothing deterred him for a moment from the work he had undertaken to do. If any man had a mission it was Mr. Hume. He had the fervour of a prophet and the enthusiasm of a fanatic held well under control by the practical insight of a statesman. And his selflessness was sublime. A man who might have become a Lieutenant-Governor was content to work silently for the people among whom he had lived so long. Now that he has been called to his rest we can only, in language all too feeble, express our undying gratitude for all that he did for us and our country with an earnestness of devotion and nobility of purpose which have scarcely any parallel."

The *Punjabee* said "his name was truly a household word, pronounced with love and veneration by the young and old. Though an official and a Mutiny veteran, he was known to the millions of Indians only as the originator of the sentiment of Indian nationality. . . . Fancy this ex-Secretary to the Government of India gathering up the scattered forces of Indians and promoting a national movement among them at a time when the echoes of the Ilbert Bill controversy had hardly died in the Himalayan fastness! He worked with a stout heart through all the discouraging and disconcerting circumstances. Never did he once quail before the huge mass of inertia that confronted him at every step."

The *Hindu*, of Madras, ranked Mr. Hume as the first of the noble band of Englishmen who after their retirement to England, keep a warm heart for India and Indians. "During the thirty-three years he came into contact with the Indian people he had conceived such a love for them that he could not bring himself to what most of his countrymen do by retiring to England and forgetting the country to which they owe so much. . . . . And of all those who, by their untiring industry, winning persuasion, and steadfast work, brought the institution into being, successfully steered it through difficulties of every kind and watched its growth vigilantly and with anxiety, Mr. Hume's name will ever be remembered with the warmest affection and gratitude."

The *Indian Patriot* regarded Mr. Hume as a "father" of the Indian people, as well as the "father" of the Congress. "If the happiness of his life was ever disturbed it was mostly on account of his earnest solicitude for India and Indians. We owe to him our love and gratitude in a measure that few other men can claim, and it behoves us to demonstrate both in the most fitting manner possible. We must erect monuments of our love and gratitude to the great man, not only in one place, but in as many places as possible, so that posterity may see how we honoured the memory of a man who, though differing in race, made himself one of us, identifying himself completely with us and with all our aims for a better state and greater contentment."

He loved India (wrote the *Wednesday Review*) as no other British statesman has loved her, and he had his reward in the willing homage of a vast population. "Who can forget the enthusiasm which he roused among the people when he visited this country nineteen years ago! His tour was a triumphal progress, and showed what even a single Englishman could do to bind the people of India closer to England and deepen their attachment to British rule. What made Mr. Hume's advice so valuable was his candour, and he never cared to whitewash in a spirit of mistaken kindness the shortcomings of the people for whom he worked."

"One of the greatest Anglo-Indians of the last century," was the opinion of the *Madras Standard*. "But for his parental care, his unceasing interest, his extraordinary exertions, his timely advice and admonitions, and his great self-sacrifice, the Indian National Congress might not have steered clear of the shoals and rocks that beset its career. To the last he remained at the helm, faithful and true, and unshaken in his belief in its strength and usefulness. He looked forward to the formation of an Indian nation, happy, contented, and manly, and a tower of strength to the British Empire. And, we have no doubt, he died with the supreme satisfaction that a mortal can have of his life's great work being fairly on the road to fruition."

The *Mahratta*, of Poona, said that Hume's memory would "be cherished in India not so much for his official career as for the work that he did after retirement in rearing a national Indian institution—the Congress. No one else could be said to have done so much as he did to foster that nursling in those days."

The *Gujarati* thought that "Providence meant to preserve his life for a great political mission, and it will be admitted on all hands that Mr. Hume did nobly fulfil the mission that had been assigned to him. Even a man like Sir William Wedderburn, with all the gentle virtues of a God-fearing Christian and high-souled Englishman, has not escaped denunciation at the hands of some of his own countrymen. It is no wonder that Mr. A. O. Hume, with his more passionate temperament and irrepressible enthusiasm, called down upon his devoted head still more fierce denunciations and even abuse at the hands of the very same critics. But he never swerved from the path he had chalked out for himself."

The *Hindi Punch* wrote that the Political Rishi of modern Bharat Land had taken his *samádhi*—the last farewell—leaving his favourite child, now a grown-up and healthy handmaid, in the service of this country. "He watched and tended the child in the cradle. He witnessed with joy the baby's toddlings. He has seen the gradual growth of the maid, and he leaves her to-day wise and strong to blow the piercing conch-shell and arouse Britannia and to beg for just rights. It is no fighting suffragette who weeps to-day for her great and good father, but a gentle spirit that roams about teaching great truths and demanding great and oft-promised rights in the interests of the Mother-country. All honour to the noble parent! India mourns the passing of a great man, and that man has an abiding haven in the expansive and grateful heart of the Motherland."

Finally, the *Beharee* held that at his grave Indians must sink all their differences, and with a feeling of enduring gratitude to him knit themselves into a united body, common heirs to a common heritage, bound together by fealty to his love of our common Motherland. "The spirit of Mr. Hume will lovingly hover over the Congress gathering of 1912; and nothing, not even the brightest and the best monument we can raise to his great and beneficent memory, will be half as pleasing to him as the union of his political heirs in maintaining the integrity and greatness of the organization which India owes to him as the greatest consequence of the British advent and occupation of the country."

Public meetings were held at all the principal cities and

towns, such as Calcutta, Bombay, Madras, Allahabad, Cawnpore, Benares, Nagpur, Bankipore, Poona, Amraoti, Yeotmal, Lucknow, Rai Bareli, Mainpuri, Meerut, Etawah, Gorakhpur, Cuddapah, Bezwada, Berhampore, Nandyal, Trichinopoly, Bapatla, and many other places. The resolutions adopted were similar in form and character, as may be judged from the telegram forwarded to Sir W. Wedderburn by the Secretaries of the Indian National Congress, which reads as follows :—

"Indians deeply mourn the death of Allan Hume. In him the country has lost its most sincere and sympathetic friend, the like of whom it may never see again, and the Congress its most beloved and esteemed founder. With unexampled energy, great perseverance and unfaltering faith he had striven amidst good report and evil to promote the social and political welfare of the people and had lived to see the firstfruits of his noble and unceasing efforts. Though it is impossible that Indians can ever repay the debt of obligation they owe to him for his righteous and disinterested service, the name of Mr. Hume will be remembered with affection and gratitude by generations to come as that of a sterling Englishman of deep and abiding sympathy with their most cherished aspirations."

The twenty-seventh Session of the Indian National Congress, held at Bankipore on December 26, 27, and 28, 1912, adopted a resolution recording "its sense of profound sorrow at the death of Allan Octavian Hume, C.B., father and founder of the Congress, to whose lifelong services, rendered at rare self-sacrifice, India feels deep and lasting gratitude, and in whose death the cause of Indian progress and reform sustained irreparable loss."

## APPENDIX V

### ETAWAH'S DEBT TO MR. HUME

(*From the "Leader," of Allahabad, August* 31, 1912)

FEW people unconnected with Etawah can understand what Mr. Hume's name means in this city and district.

A brief narration of facts pertaining to his administration of the district will be an interesting reading and remind many of the name and glory he had already won as an able and sympathetic administrator long, long before he figured as a political leader.

The history of Etawah is inseparably associated with his name, and his memory will ever be cherished in the grateful hearts of its residents. He was a young man hardly twenty-six when he was put in charge of the responsible and onerous duties of the collector and magistrate of the district. A born administrator, endowed with a clear foresight, strong personality, determined will, undaunted courage, God-fearing, and indefatigable, he soon made his influence felt throughout the district and came to be respected and loved by the rich and poor alike. Peace, progress and reform followed his administration. There was "nothing but hopefulness and peace" in Etawah, when suddenly the Mutiny broke out. The condition of the district preceding the dark days of the Mutiny is thus very vividly described by Mr. Hume in his characteristic lucid and forcible style :—

"Never apparently had the prospects of the district been so cheering ; crime was, and had been for the previous two years, steadily decreasing; the revenue flowed in without the necessity of recourse to a single coercive process; public libraries and numerous schools gave rich promise of future progress; new lines of communication were being rapidly opened out, the railroad was fast opening; the great canal, with its daily multiplying branches, steadily diffused fertility, through an ever-widening area, and all classes of the community, though not of course without their minor grievances, were on the whole singularly happy and contented. Suddenly the Mutiny burst upon us, effacing apparently in a day the labour of years" (p. 148 of the *Gazetteer*). With the spread of the Mutiny in the neighbouring district the situation here became extremely critical. Mr. Hume's energetic measures, wise counsel, determined attitude, with which the history of the district is replete, dispersed and quieted down the rebels; and "in a few days the most perfect order was restored." During his temporary absence which the subsequent circumstances and his own "prostration with cholera" had forced upon him, he "kept up a continuous correspondence with the Indian officials and the well-disposed zemindars, communicating news and orders, deciding all difficult points referred to him, and endeavouring by proclamations and letters to keep alive every feeling of loyalty to the State." And even those who were rebelliously inclined were kept within bound by letters from Mr. Hume. He had been as anxious to return as his loyal and faithful officials and zemindars were to have him back. On his way back he learnt that no detachment had been, as was ordered by the Government, left behind by Brigadier Walpole, but "nothing daunted, Mr. Hume and his escort pushed on and reoccupied the station." His gallant dash at Anant Ram, the action at Harchandpore and numerous other skirmishes are still described in glowing terms. These point to his having been at the early age of twenty-eight as good a general and as great a statesman as any country might well be proud of. On July 2, 1858, Mr. Hume again fell ill and had to be relieved. That *very* day the rebel Raja whom he had already crushed before again raised his head. A period of unrest followed when he rejoined from leave and restored peace. This is a very striking example of his strong personality. A glance at the history of the period forcibly reminds one of another prominent trait of his character—his judicious selection of men and his unbounded confidence in their loyalty. Raja Lachman Singh, then a kumar, Munshis Debi Prasad, Ishwari Prasad, Ram Bakhsh, tehsildars, and Munshi Shiam Bihari Lal, Kotwal, among the officials, and Rao Jaswant Rao, K. Zar Singh of Partabner, L. Laik Singh of Marchandpore, Lal Chatur Singh of Sahar, Rao Jawahar Singh of Barhpura, the Raja of Malajani, the Bagpais of Lukhna, the Tewaris of Kudarkat, the rais of Takah and Babu Ajudhia Prasad of Etawah, *all Hindus*, were his faithful allies and were conspicuous for their loyalty. To each and all mutineers and loyalists he had but one reply—" It may be months, it may be years, but sooner or later the English Government will get the upper hand and every man will eat the fruit of his deeds." Memorable words indeed! They reveal intense sympathy and true loyalty. The two feelings are very happily blended, each overlapping the other. We leave Mr. Hume to describe with just pride the result of his just and wise policy and its moral effect upon those who came under the spell of his magnetic personality. "From the very day," he wrote, "I first at the borders of the district received the congratulatory visits of hundreds of our well-wishers, I gave it to be generally understood that I had no feelings of animosity to gratify. . . . The enemies of order had, even in the worst of times, always been in a minority, numerically speaking, but from the time that my intentions became generally known they certainly on the mainland parganas (excluding Auriya) scarcely exceeded 1 per cent. of the population. In this lay our strength, any surprise by the ill-affected and their mutineer friends was impossible; every move, every accession of strength, was reported at once from a dozen different quarters; men—nay whole communities—who had been plundering, were, instead of being goaded into rebellion, led to return to their peaceful pursuits and to submit to arbitration the adjustment of the costs of their transgression." The *Gazetteer* sums up Mr. Hume's career in the following telling words : "Few districts in the province can compare with Etawah for the loyalty of its inhabitants during the great rebellion. This was owing to the kindly feeling entertained towards Mr. Hume by the majority of the people and to the persevering efforts made by him to keep alive those feelings. . . . To Mr. Hume nearly all the credit is due. Etawah owes much to that distinguished officer, Mr. A. O. Hume, C.B., for many years collector of the district. It was largely owing to his influence that the Mutiny disturbances left so slight a mark upon it, and his name still lingers gratefully in the memories of the people."

The Mutiny over, Mr. Hume devoted his untiring energy primarily towards the extension of education. Seven tahsil schools were opened. More than two hundred and fifty village schools were recognized and aid began to be given from the public funds. Hume High School, the chief school of the district, was raised by him to the status of a superior Zilla school. The structure of the school building is architecturally interesting. It consists of a fine hall supported in the centre by an enormous arch, and flanked on either side by two high and spacious rooms. Running round the entire building are long and roomy corridors. The original building before the extensions on the north and the south sides was in the form of an H. The entire cost of construction amounted to Rs. 34,000, out of which Rs. 24,000 were subscribed by Mr. Hume himself and the residents of the district. As long as he was collector of the district Mr. Hume paid a monthly subscription of Rs. 30 towards its support, but on leaving the district he presented it with a donation of Rs. 7200, invested in Government paper, calculated to yield from interest an amount equal to the monthly subscription he had paid till then. From the sum annually accruing four scholarships of Rs. 6 per mensem each are awarded to the four best boys of the middle section under fourteen years of age, for proficiency either in English or mathematics. In addition to this Mr. Hume made a separate endowment of Rs. 1200 for an annual prize to be given to the youngest boy who passed the entrance examination.

The first medical institution built in Etawah was built in 1856 by Mr. A. O. Hume.

Old Etawah lies among or at the head of the ravines, and the newer portions of the city stretch backwards to the north. Several *nalas* intersect the site of the town. Owing to the uneven nature of the ground, communication between the old and the new quarters was difficult before the time of Mr. Hume. But by means of cuttings, embankments and bridges he made fine broad metalled roads, and rendered communication at all times easy or practicable. He made so many good roads that even after forty-five years of his leaving Etawah, with all the municipal and district boards' arrangements, only very few roads have been constructed since.

In the centre of the city is Humeganj. Formerly the place was an unsightly and uneven piece of waste ground infested with wild beasts, but it was levelled and drained by Mr. Hume and it now forms the site of imposing public buildings and a handsome market-place also called the Humeganj, the principal grain and cotton market which is lined with handsome shops, remarkable for their fine brickwork arches. To the west of the grain market is Hume's Serai, which is entered by a handsome gateway resembling a triumphal arch. The imposing building of the Tehsili, the American Mission Church, which is now used as municipal office, the vegetable market, Hume High School, the Kotwali, the old Munsifi and the town school and the hospital, all stand upon the site and will ever remain a living monument of Mr. Hume and his work in Etawah. He also erected a *baradari* on the débris of Somersah's fortress and constructed a road leading to it, which is now out of order. The handsome residence of the collector and the small building used as a club were also built by him in the peculiar style of architecture which characterized all Mr. Hume's constructions. It was not only the city which received his attention, but the whole district bears testimony to his kind and loving regards and the real improvements effected by him. There is also a Humeganj in Phapund. Another Humeganj, consisting of a large, well-kept square, with a central metalled roadway and masonry shops, adorns Auriya.

I leave it to you and your readers to see for yourselves what claims Etawah has on the proposed Provincial Hume Memorial, and how far it would be in the fitness of things to perpetuate his memory at a place where he is already so much respected. The educative effect of such a memorial on the residents of Etawah and of the neighbouring districts would be immense. These places are admittedly still lingering behind in the onward march. They ought to receive due attention from those whose main study is to see that none lags behind. If the suggestion is favourably countenanced other details would be easily forthcoming.

ZORAWAR SINGH NIGAM
(*Municipal Commissioner, Etawah*).